# Freedom from My Self

# Freedom from My Self

## Moving beyond the voice in my head

Craig J Mabie

Copyright © 2015 Craig J Mabie

All rights reserved. No part of the book may be transmitted or reproduced by any form or means, either mechanical or electronic, including recording and photocopying, or by any known storage and retrieval system, without permission in writing from the Publisher, except in the case of short quotations being used in a review.

This book is designed to provide information and motivation to readers. It is sold with the understanding that the author is not engaged to render any type of psychological, legal, or any other kind of professional advice. The content is the sole expression and opinion of its author. No warranties or guarantees are expressed or implied by the publisher's choice to include any of the content in this volume. Neither the publisher nor the individual author shall be liable for any physical, psychological, emotional, financial, or commercial damages, including, but not limited to, special, incidental, consequential or other damages. Our views and rights are the same: You are responsible for your own choices, actions, and results.

This is a work of creative nonfiction. The events are portrayed to the best of Craig J Mabie's memory. While all the stories in this book are true, names have been omitted and some identifying details have been changed to protect the privacy of the people involved.

ISBN: 978-0-9863345-0-4 Paperback

ISBN: 978-0-9863345-1-1 Hardback

ISBN: 978-0-9863345-2-8 Ebook

Cover Design: Douglas Sutherland

Publishing Consultants: Pickawoowoo Publishing Group


UpThrust Publishing

www.upthrustpublishing.com

www.freedomfrommyself.net

Printed in the United States of America

# Dedicated to ...

The Sunapee, White, Green, Rocky, Sierra Nevada, Wrangell, Alps and Cascade mountains, as well as to all the people who have uplifted me.

# Contents

The Golden Child ................................ | 1
The Descent ...................................... | 5
Slap, Smack, Snap ............................. | 22
Queer Adam in the Winter ................ | 33
Out and About? ................................ | 45
Lost ................................................... | 69
No Moonlight in Vermont .................. | 87
Colorado ........................................... | 118
Vocal Cords ...................................... | 142
The Crux ........................................... | 183
Big Wood River ................................. | 208
Awakening ........................................ | 227
Appendix .......................................... | 262
References ........................................ | 264

# The Golden Child

I raised my arms high into the air and shook my hands violently. I walked out onto the deck and was so astonished by what I saw, that my nervous habit erupted. The intense ball of nervous energy that had exploded within me had to be released somehow, and my oscillating hands were on fire as they reached for the sky. The surge of vivacity that the scene before me had initiated was squelched quickly as I heard my mother say, "Hands down Craig, Hands Down!"

My *arms raised, hands shaking, nervous habit* was repressed by my mother's command. I slowly lowered my arms to my side, and held my hands tight against my thighs – a technique that I had learned in order to control my nervous habit. But still, the energy surged within me as I witnessed the scene.

Splayed out before me was my birthday party, celebrating my fifth year of life. The warm spring sun shone down on the outdoor deck of our house and illuminated the cornucopia of presents, cakes, hats, confetti, balloons and people. The light of midday caught shiny ribbons and bows, and tiny bursts of light filled the deck space. Lying across the deck chairs, picnic table and benches was a mountain of presents. A literal sea of birthday gifts spread across the deck – too numerous for my five year old brain to comprehend. The brilliant colors of the carefully wrapped packages filled up my eyes and sent waves of anticipation and excitement through my body.

My mother and grandmother had planned and executed an extraordinary birthday event for me. It was over the top in every manner and I spent the afternoon experiencing sheer joy. The kind of joy that a five year old boy can experience when opening gift after gift after gift – so many gifts that it took the entire afternoon to open them all! The kind of joy that limitless cake, ice cream and all sorts of additional birthday confections can provide. The kind of joy that can come from being the absolute center of attention and focus, of all the kids and adults at the birthday party.

This birthday party was a microcosm of my early life. I was the *Golden Child*!

I was my parent's only child and the only boy – the only son. My mother was an only child as well. As a result, I was *the* focus of my mother and my mother's mother. They showered me with attention, love, gifts, and experiences.

My grandmother built me a Christmas train, the cars overflowing with gifts, which filled the living room every Christmas. My parents sent me on chaperoned trips to Disneyland and Disney World. My dad bought me a BB gun and a mini bike; I motored through the woods shooting at any target I could find. He taught me to hunt and took me on hunting trips. My grandfather had a large farm where I camped, hiked and fished.

# The Golden Child

My parents had a speedboat that plowed the waters of Lake Sunapee, and many an hour of my young life was spent on the water. The boat was a Chris-Craft – a unique kind of watercraft that was characterized by a shiny, deep red mahogany wood hull. We would begin our day on the water by walking to the wooden boathouse where the Ring-a-Ding Ding, the name my parents gave to this glorious craft, would float in storage, just waiting for us. Every time I stepped into that boat house I was transfixed by the play of light. Sunshine would shaft in through the open door of the boathouse and reflect off the glassy, polished mahogany finish of the boat and combine with the reflected light from the crystal clear water. Streaks of flashy, shining light would dash all around the interior of the boat house, illuminating the space and creating an ethereal, northern lights type of phenomenon. I would watch the reflected light dance across the faces of my parents as they began to load the boat with our provisions for the day. The gyration of light in this space filled me with energy, and seared a memory of pure ecstasy into my young brain.

And then there were the sounds of the boathouse. The gentle rocking slosh of the lake water as it lapped against the hull of the boat and the pylons supporting the boathouse. The creak emanating from the bumpers as the boat edge and the tie-up pilings struck one another. The hollow, amplified sound of our voices echoing off the old wood of the enclosed boathouse. And then, the most exciting sound of all – my father starting the engine. Chris-Crafts are constructed in such a way that the engine produces a unique, signature sound. Deep, throaty, basal reverberations emanated from below the floorboards in the stern of the boat. My dad would rev the engine to warm it up and the substratal vibrations would flow up through the bottom of the boat and into my body. The combination of the lights, sounds and feelings in that boathouse transported me to a glorious world of joy – and we hadn't even left the dock yet!

My dad would gently shift the engine into reverse and the boat would ease out of the boathouse and into the open waters of Lake Sunapee. The waters of Lake Sunapee cast a spell. In a state containing numerous glacially carved and spring fed lakes, the waters of Lake Sunapee stand out as some of the clearest and purest. I would gaze over the side of the boat and marvel at how far down into the water I could see. The transparent liquid beckoned me to join it. And join it I did – with fervor. My day was spent immersed in the elixir of Sunapee's waters. My joy was palpable.

As a young boy, I was presented with wondrous experiences such as these. I was a lucky kid – the Golden Child.

This was the way of my world and then, at the end of the fourth grade school year, my parents told me that we were moving. They said that we were going to live in a new town about an hour's drive away from where we were living. Moving was something we had done before. A new adventure was about to begin.

# The Descent

## Avoidance

When you are a kid you just find yourself in a place.

It was the summer of 1973, and we had just moved into our new house in this small, rural New Hampshire town. It was a warm, bright day and our neighborhood was throwing its annual block party. This new neighborhood was an isolated sort of place, with one circular drive and two crossroads, fifty or so houses, surrounded on all sides by deep New Hampshire woods

I ran out the back door of our house with both hesitation and excitement, headed for the block party and this new world. When I arrived, sporting games were in full swing and I could not believe how many neighborhood boys of my age were lined up for the high jump. As I watched, they were all clearing the bar with ease. I joined the line and when it became my turn I ran and jumped, attempting to clear the bar. My fat, uncoordinated body hit the bar and fell into a heap on the ground. All the boys looked at me and began to laugh. I heard, "Who is that fat new kid?" I got up, embarrassed to my core and retreated quickly back to my house. I had been introduced to the neighborhood boys and the stage had been set.

I had never been involved in sports. It was not part of my parent's world, and therefore it had not been a part of mine. No Little League, soccer, basketball, football, etc. By the time I reached the summer after fourth grade, we had moved to and lived in five different towns in New Hampshire. There had not been a lot of time to join in with a community of kids, sporting or otherwise; I had led a rather solitary life with regard to peers. My dad was a hunter and, by association, I had become a child of the woods. I was an emotional, feeling and intuitive kid, and I was most at home when out experiencing the forests of New Hampshire.

This new neighborhood was a shock. There were ten or more boys my age living there, all in close proximity. They had lived there all their lives. They were team sports aficionados and were deeply involved in team sports culture.

It took me a while to venture out into the neighborhood again after the block party incident, but one day I found myself out on the street as the neighborhood boys were organizing a kickball game. They told me that I needed to play and I was assigned to a team. It was my turn to kick and the ball came rolling toward me. Lumbering and uncoordinated, I kicked with all my might, completely missed the ball and fell to the ground. Laughter from the boys ensued, then ridicule. One of the boys had learned that my last name was *Mabie* (pronounced Maybe), and my first name calling moniker was shouted out by him, "Mabie the Baby." I was asked to no longer be on the team because I was no good.

I spent the remainder of the summer trying to avoid those

boys. It was not an easy thing to do as the neighborhood was close knit and isolated. Over the course of the summer the boys had branded and labeled me as a fat, uncoordinated and non-athletic outsider. A person easy to ridicule. When school started in the fall, avoiding them was not possible.

## Mabie the Baby

All the kids walked to the elementary school which was just down the street from the neighborhood. We had to walk to school at the same time in the morning and I became the butt of their jokes during the walk, setting the stage for the school day.

Recess was the worst because it meant team sports on the playground. Tetherball, baseball, basketball, kickball – I was hopelessly bad at all of them. One particular recess kickball game stands out in my mind. As the teams were picked the boys from my neighborhood indicated that I was no good, and I was chosen last. This humiliation was the first of many. The person up to kick before me, from the other team, was a young girl. She had the reputation of being able to kick the ball far, and as a result all the field players moved back into the field in anticipation of her big kick. She did not disappoint. She kicked the ball far over everyone's head, and then she sailed around the bases scoring a point. Everyone cheered.

I was up next. As I stood there preparing to kick, one of the neighborhood boys yelled, "Mabie the Baby is up, everybody move in!" I watched as all the kids moved in towards me, as close as they could get, anticipating a short kick or, even worse, a complete miss. I cannot describe to you how pronounced the memory and the feeling of that moment became. Those kids *moving in on me* represented what was happening in my world. I felt pressure, anxiety, lack – *fear*. I felt as though I, quite simply, was not good enough. Not only at kickball, but, as a very impressionable fifth grader, my mind was beginning to take me on a journey toward not being good at anything.

Everyone was watching as the ball came rolling towards me. I kicked, and completely missed the ball. I heard, "Figures," "Told ya so," "Mabie the Baby," "Next time he has to be on your team," from the kids. I retreated to the side of the school building, alone, feeling some safety with my back against the warm brick of the structure. I remember wishing with all my might that the recess bell would ring so this hell would end.

The hell did not end, it had just begun. When the school bell rang at the end of the day, it was time to walk home to the neighborhood – along with all the other boys. It was here that my first experience with potential bodily harm occurred. One of the boys was an athletic, powerfully built kid who had a big personality. He liked to be physical, and he had decided that I was the right person over whom to exercise his prowess. I represented the perfect opportunity for him to impress his peers and enhance his reputation. He was the kind of kid that got a high from dominating and impressing others. He had a huge ego, and I became his target. On the walk home from school that day, in front of all the boys, he challenged me to a fist fight. He said that the fight would be the next day, after school and in the woods between the neighborhood and the school.

## The Descent

I now understood a new level of fear. I understood that I was no match for this kid, had no idea how to fist fight and that this fight would be a complete and utter humiliation for me in front of all the neighborhood and school kids. I understood that all the kids would be in support of my adversary. I also understood that I could be physically injured.

The memories of that night at home are seared into my brain. I had to think of a way out of the fist fight. The fear was intense and was an incredible motivator for me. Think, think, and think. There had to be a way out.

That night I discovered the capability of my *thinking mind*. I devised a plan to appeal to my adversary's ego and hopefully diffuse the situation. On the next afternoon, the end of the school day bell rang. The atmosphere was charged; there was much anticipation of the fight. Many boys gathered around me and my opponent as we started walking toward the woods. I felt and witnessed their support for him as we walked. I had a deep, primal fear of annihilation as I realized that it was not just me against my combatant, but me against the entire pack of boys. I knew that I had absolutely no chance.

During this walk I somehow gathered the strength to implement the plan that I had conceived the night before. I was going to verbally appeal to his sense of strength and his need to be in control and to dominate – his need to impress. I built my adversary up by telling him that he was strong and I was weak. I told him that he was an excellent fighter so why in the world would he waste his effort on weak and incapable little me? I told him that there would be no fight because I would just succumb to his prowess. He didn't need to fight me because it would be a waste of his time. I told him that there was no one in school who could stand up to him because he was so powerful and competent. I appealed to his need to impress by describing him as a larger than life superkid in front of all his peers.

He stopped walking. He placed his hands against my shoulders and pushed me hard. He said to the rest of the boys, "Come on, let's get out of here, he's not worth it." He walked off toward the woods, the rest of the boys in tow, leaving me there on the playground. Somehow, my verbal positioning had resonated with him and my strategy had worked. I remember standing there watching them walk away and experiencing an intense soup of emotions; fear, relief, humiliation. I could not move until I realized, very suddenly, that I had a chance to escape and I had better take it. The only thing that I remember about the walk home was the intense need to look back over my shoulder to make sure that my adversary and the pack of boys had not changed their minds.

## **ACE**

The elementary school was dominated by boys that played team sports. The neighborhood boys were part of that group and they had all been involved in team sports with each other since the first grade. My experience with kickball translated to all the other team sports that I was forced to participate in. I was never taught how to play these sports, did not know how to play them and had no interest in playing them. That, combined with my lack of physical coordination and heavy-set body, contributed greatly to my failure at any team sport in which I was forced to take part. It came to pass that I was always chosen last when picking teams and frequently heard the words, "Oh no, not Mabie the Baby. Not on our team!" Team sports became an intense source of humiliation for me; a place of deep fear as I experienced rejection, negative judgment and isolation.

The intensity of this fear boiled over during one particular event. I remember being in school one day and being told that during the next school day, at gym period, there was going to be a boys flag football game on the playground. A spike of terror filled my heart. Flag football, what was that? I didn't know how to play football. I'd never even heard of *flag* football. What I did know was that my required participation in this team sport would end up being an episode of intense humiliation for me. I would be chosen last for a team, rejected and ridiculed. During the rest of that school day my mind was filled with dread, anticipating the carnage that the next day would bring.

That night at home, I once again discovered the capability of my thinking mind. Think, think, think. There had to be a way out. Should I go to my parents? No, that was untenable. My dad was a very macho, forceful, demanding and powerful sort of guy. He had little emotional availability, an enormous and robust personality as well as a large and intimidating physical presence. He believed that instilling the fear of his wrath in his children was the most effective parenting technique. The fear of his wrath would keep me from doing anything wrong. As such, I was terrified of my father and could not dream of approaching him with this problem, or with any problem for that matter. I felt that I would be judged as a sissy, weak, incapable or not good enough, and I was already experiencing too much of this from my peers. Going to my mother was not an option. I did not trust that she would not let my father know what was going on. My mother had been raised an only child in a small town in New Hampshire where her father was an upper-middle-class, prominent business man. She had been treated like a queen her entire life – she was the apple of her father's eye. She had grown up as a protected child of privilege and therefore, at some level deep in my young psyche, I must have convinced myself that she was incapable of understanding or relating to what I was currently going through. My mother cared for me and loved me and I knew this. I felt though, that she would not have been capable of handling my problems on her own, and she would have needed to seek the help of my father.

In addition, my father was very unavailable to me because he was devoting most of his time and energy into a new retail home improvement business that he had started. This new business was the catalyst for our move to this small New Hampshire town. He worked long hours at the business; a grueling Monday to Friday work week, Tuesday and Thursday evenings and Saturdays as well as out of town travel. Money was very important and highly prized by my father and he saw this business as the ticket to his success. He poured his heart and soul into it. He was, quite simply, too busy to know what was going on with me during this time. This fact, in concert with the fear that

## The Descent

I had of my father, created a powerful force within me that prevented me from approaching him with my problems.

I was the only child from my parents (my dad had two daughters from a previous marriage that were much older and had already left the house) and the only son. I had received the message from my family that there were expectations for me to be something quite special because I was the *only son* and the one to carry on the family name. I was the Golden Child! That message was not congruent with what was currently happening in my life. For all these reasons I felt that help from my parents was not an option. This was a feeling that would go on for many years.

That night, thinking about my flag football dilemma, I conjured my escape. I would fake injury! I went to the medicine cabinet in our house and started looking for a way to feign injury. There, right in front of me on the second shelf, appeared my salvation. An ACE bandage. I will pretend that I have a sprained ankle. You can't play flag football with a sprained ankle, right? I took the bandage and hid it carefully in my room, to be retrieved the next morning before the walk to school.

The school bell rang announcing the period for gym class. Proceeding down the school hallway, toward the gym and my date with flag football humiliation, I ducked into the boy's bathroom. There, I entered a stall, pulled out the carefully concealed ACE bandage from my pocket and proceeded to wrap my left ankle with the bandage. I had never wrapped an ankle before. It was difficult to do and when I was done it did not look right. "Is this how a doctor would do it?" I thought to myself. As I realized that I did not possess the skill to wrap the ankle in a way that looked convincing I was overcome with angst. Was my perfect plan unraveling just like the bandage on my ankle? Was I going to have to play flag football? The thought of having to try to play created such fear in me that my motivation to wrap it convincingly became strong. Again and again I wrapped it, trying to make it look like a professional job. The final bell for gym class rang; I had run out of time. The way I had it wrapped, the way it looked, would have to do. It was time to exit the bathroom stall, walk down the hall and put on my show. With a slight limp, I entered the gym. All the other boys were busy attaching flags to their hips, preparing for the game. The gym teacher was assisting with the preparations and I knew that I had to present my injury to him and request permission to sit out the game. What would be his reaction? Would he be fooled? Would he request to see the ankle? Would he send me to the school nurse for an examination? Would my cover be blown? Would the school nurse call my parents, tell them about my sprained ankle and then listen to them say, "What sprained ankle?" What would my father then do?

As I walked (limped) toward the gym teacher I was filled with anxiety. It is hard to describe the elementary school age angst that I was feeling in those moments during that walk. My whole body tingled, focusing down to an intense sense of heat in my abdomen. The taste of sour bile was in my throat and a feeling of deep pressure was present in my lungs. I was experiencing intense fear.

I pointed to the ACE bandage around my ankle and said to the gym teacher, "I sprained my ankle so I can't play." He said nothing. It felt like an eternity as he stared at my wrapped ankle – speechless. At that very moment, I became so lost in my intensely thinking mind that I was paralyzed from movement or speech. Why was he not saying anything? Was he buying it? *Say something*, Mr. Gym Teacher! All of a sudden he uttered, "Does it hurt?" I had to reach very deep to find a response and all that came out was, "Yes." Silence again, for what seemed like an eternity. He was looking at me now, and my interpretation of his look was that of suspicion. I was filled with doubt. How could I have possibly thought that I could have fooled an adult gym teacher? He is on to me, and fear of his wrath welled up inside me and became almost as great as my fear of playing flag football. I felt a tear forming in my eye.

"You go outside and sit along the side of the field and watch the game," he said with a suspicious, wary look. It had worked. I had dodged the bullet, or so I thought. What I did not realize, and had not thought of, was that I would be explaining and answering questions about my sprained ankle during the entire time of the flag football game. Sitting there on the side of the field, my non-participation in the game was glaringly obvious. Kids came up to me and asked, "Why are you not playing?", "How did you sprain your ankle?" I made up a story in response, but all I felt was wary suspicion from all of my peers. The game ended, as did the school day, and I started walking (limping) home. I entered through the downstairs door of the house, quickly removed the ACE bandage from my ankle and concealed it in my clothing before walking up the stairs to greet my mother. She asked me how school was today. I said, "Fine."

Craig J Mabie

## Withdrawal

I became a recluse. My sanctuary, or my prison, depending on how you look at it, was the basement family room of my house. The room was safe, a place to hide. Television became my world. *The Price Is Right*, Cartoons, *$10,000 Pyramid* – TV was an escape. It was a place to be free of the trauma of the neighborhood boys outside. I can remember listening for them. Are they out there? Are they playing team sports in the street? When I would hear them the dread would overtake me. I would go to the window, open the curtain just enough to be able to look outside and confirm the source of my fear. There they were with their baseballs, kickballs, and soccer balls – just waiting to annihilate Mabie the Baby. I quickly adjusted the curtain to ensure a full window block and retreated back to my TV. "Why don't you go outside and play," rang my mother's voice from upstairs. "It is such a beautiful day and all the kids are outside playing," would be her follow up statement. My reply would be, "As soon as I finish watching this show."

The fear of walking outside into the presence of that pack of neighborhood boys was crippling. I knew what was in store for me if I did. I became a master at peering through the basement windows to find my opportunity for escape. When they were down the street and just out of sight, when they were called in for lunch, when they got in the car to go off to their team sporting practices and events – those were my opportunities. From behind the curtains, I could identify these windows of escape. The route, the trajectory, the quickest path into the obscurity of the woods – all this I determined from that sliver of space in the parted

## The Descent

curtain. Then, when I was as sure as I could be, I opened the basement door and headed out into the light. I can remember the intensity of my heart beat, heavy with the fear that my calculations were incorrect and I would have a confrontation with the boys. Scanning the surrounding neighborhood, was I right? Was the coast clear? Could I make it to the woods? Dread. Then, relief! A free passage to the woods. I scrambled as fast as my uncoordinated and overweight body would allow, and crossed the threshold into the New Hampshire forest.

Obscurity, Freedom, Quiet, Peace, Tranquility, Safety! This is what the woods provided for me. Travelling from the neighborhood to the woods was to transition to a different world. A world free of burden and full of the possibilities of unhindered exploration. There was a brook in the forest that became my very close friend. I spent hours watching it, fishing in it, exploring it, damning it and building my sanctuary (some would call it a fort) on its banks. On the hillside above the brook there was a clearing where I would sit and take in the peace of the natural world. Out in the distance I could see the mountains of New Hampshire and they called to me. I began to dream. I remember, clearly, a light igniting inside of me – I wanted to explore those peaks. You don't need to know how to play team sports to climb mountains, right? Maybe there was something *athletic* that I could do that would not involve a pack of marauding boys. I felt hope. Then, in an instant, it was gone and the reality of being a fifth grader set in. I had no way of getting to those mountains and, it was dinner time. Time to go to the edge of the woods and sight and determine a clear line of egress from the forest and ingress to the house. A line that would be free of detection from the neighborhood boys.

Sunday nights were the worst. My mind would spin with fearful thoughts of the morning walk to school and the subsequent school day. The morning walks to school were not chaperoned by adults. In rural New Hampshire in the early 1970's, the general feeling was that it was safe for elementary school age children to make this kind of walk on their own. Free and unencumbered by adults, the neighborhood boys would have their cruel fun with *Mabie the Baby*. Pushing, shoving, knocking my books and papers out of my hand, stealing my school supplies, verbal taunting – it was all part of my walk to school.

On one particular Sunday night I devised a plan to try to eliminate this walking to school trauma from my life. I concocted a story which I delivered to my parents that evening. I told them that I was getting to school ten minutes early each day and that I did not need to leave so early in the morning in order to walk to school and arrive on time. They bought it! I must have had a good delivery – fear was such a powerful motivator for me. The next morning I employed my well honed craft of peering through a slit in the basement window curtain, and determined when the pack of boys started their walk to school. Once they were sufficiently down the road so as not to be able to notice me walking behind them, I hit the road. It worked like a dream. A peaceful, non-traumatic walk to school.

## It's a Cold

Until I got to school, that is. By now, a substantial *force* was building in the elementary school. A force empowered by multiple kids sharing a common idea. The neighborhood boys had communicated very effectively with many other kids in school concerning the attributes and circumstances of this *Mabie the Baby* kid. To the other kids in school, they talked about my lack of sporting prowess, my fat and uncoordinated body, my *fake* ankle sprain, my inability to fight, my loner tendencies and my complete lack of popularity. It is well known that kids can be cruel, and the neighborhood boys were on a roll, spreading cruel notions of me to all their peers in the elementary school.

The *force* that this created resulted in my isolation, rejection and humiliation at school. It was Valentine's Day and all the kids at school were busy making Valentine's Day cards for classmates. I saw this as an opportunity to win some friends and support among my peers, so I put great time and effort into making Valentine's Day cards for all the members of my class. When it came time to distribute the cards, I enthusiastically travelled around the classroom placing my cards into each kid's card basket that was perched on their desk. Finally, a way to connect and communicate with my classmates – it was a very good feeling.

I returned to my seat, peered into my Valentine's Day card basket that was perched on my desk, and abruptly felt that very good feeling being replaced with a feeling of unease, rejection and humiliation. There was not one Valentine's Day card in my basket. Not a single one. The neighborhood boy's campaign against me had been very effective. I was the class loser, the one to ridicule, the one to exclude.

I sat in my chair, stunned, and all I could do was plot how I was going to avoid the boys on the walk home at the end of the school day. The end of the day came and I noticed that a Valentines' Day card had appeared in my basket. I opened it and saw that it was from the teacher. The end of the day bell rang, I went to the bathroom, entered a stall, closed the door and, very quietly so that no one would hear, sobbed with a deep desperation that I did not understand.

It was all too much and once again my mind was plotting how to escape. I had caught a cold and needed to stay home from school for a day. What a relief it was to not be in that school environment. I discovered that the sore throat, stuffy nose and headache were infinitely more palatable than the circumstances that I faced at school. Sickness was going to be my next avenue of relief! The symptoms of the cold would keep me home for a day or two, but I devised an act to convince my mother that the illness carried on. I managed to stay home for an entire week. A week of television in the basement with no kids outside during the day – *Nirvana*!

I did not anticipate the ramifications at school. Once I returned from my "illness", not only did I face the old familiar elementary school circumstances, but there was the added pressure of having fallen behind academically. Catch up was a bitch and added to the pressure. Still, the relief from school was so great that faking sickness became *my* game plan. I used it frequently during the fifth and sixth grade. Looking back, it is astounding that I was not held back a grade due to the amount of school that I missed. There was an additional price, however, that came with my game plan. As a result of missing so much school, I was placed into the *slower* kids group in the classroom. It was an academic humiliation that drove a wound deep inside me. Missing school, as well as all the trauma that I was experiencing in the school environment, affected my ability to perform academically. My mind did not see it that way though. Rather, my thoughts internalized more insecurity, more self doubt and reinforced the notion that I was not good enough.

By the time sixth grade had arrived, the trauma of my world in this new town was firmly imbedded in me, and I was seeking relief.

I saw him in the gymnasium on the first day of the sixth grade and I knew that he was a new kid in town. Something attracted me to him and, very uncharacteristically for me, I approached him, introduced myself and set out to make him my friend. It was one of the best things that I ever could have done for myself. One of the best choices I ever made. The friendship blossomed and grew. He was not like the other boys that had come to rock my world. He was not aggressive, mean or antagonistic. He was mild, calm, introverted and intelligent. He was not a team sports person. He lived in a different neighborhood which provided me a place to escape from the traumas of my own. He would be the one peer in my life that would bring joy, happiness and friendship to my world over the next several years. He became my best friend. On that day that we met in the sixth grade, we set out on quite a journey together; a journey of discovery that would not fully manifest until we became older.

# Slap, Smack, Snap

## Middle School

Finally, the summer between sixth and seventh grade arrived. The summer brought tremendous relief. I implemented all the strategies that I had developed over the past two years to avoid the neighborhood boys. As a result, I had freedom to explore the woods and attain some peace in my young life. It was all good until August first. August first – that means the summer is half over. That means school will start in a month! In my head, the summer had started to end when in reality it was only half over. I cannot understate the dread that the thought of the new school year brought to my mind and body. Especially *this* new school year. You see, my time at the elementary school had ended and it was time to move to the middle school. The middle school was several miles away and involved what to me was an experience that held the biggest potential yet for personal trauma – a bus ride to school. I had to take a bus to school with the other neighborhood boys. No more walking to school late to avoid the pack of kids. My mind could not come up with a way to avoid the interaction. I had to be at that bus stop and take that bus ride with those boys – there was just no way around it. My interaction with them would increase exponentially. That was only the half of it – there was also the bus ride home.

The suffering that accompanies such fear and anxiety was with me for the month of August. My mind and emotions were in complete control of my being. The only word that I can find that comes anywhere close to how I was feeling, a word that I have and will continue to use in this story, is *dread*.

## The (very) Wrong Way

September came and so did the bus rides. My strategy was to be as quiet and unobtrusive as possible at both the bus stop and on the bus. I figured that if I made myself as small as possible, the chances of attracting attention to me would be less and the potential for bullying would be reduced. It didn't work.

Sitting on the bus one day I remember hearing the words from behind me, "Hey, look, it's Mabie the Baby." I froze with fear and sat motionless, hoping that nothing else would occur. I had recognized the voice as belonging to one of the boys in the neighborhood. Then, I felt it – a hit across the back of my head. A slap, a whack – followed by a sting of physical pain and, worse, a deep stab of emotional pain and fear. I was absolutely paralyzed, then, another hit. Similar in strike and force but this time followed by laughter. Growing laughter. A chorus of laughter. My attacker was smart; he was hitting me in a manner where the bus driver could not see what was going on. When the laughter erupted I could see the face of the bus driver as she looked into her viewing mirror, but by the time she looked the assault had already occurred and she saw nothing. I don't remember how many hits I endured on that ride, I just remember being completely frozen by fear until the bus arrived at the school, stopped and allowed for my escape.

The middle school was small, consisting of one hallway leading to a few classrooms, a gymnasium and offices. In my town, it was where the kids went to seventh and eighth grade. It was in an isolated spot, far from any commercial or residential development and was surrounded by woods and marsh. Team sports were a huge part of the culture and the gymnasium was a busy place. Gym class was a big deal. I was introduced to a new world – the world of the locker room and showers. By the seventh grade, some of the boys were growing physically bigger and were experiencing puberty. I was not one of them, I was small, fat and my body was still very childlike. This was more fertile ground for bullying.

During one particular gym class, we played a basketball game. It seemed as if all the kids knew how to play basketball. How did they learn? Who taught them? I did not know how to play basketball. Teams were picked and as had become the custom, I was chosen last. I knew this – one of the primary objectives of the game was to dribble the ball to the end of the court and get the ball in the basket. At one point in the game the ball came to me. My mind told me that this action was the result of one of the following: the opposite team passed the ball to me because they knew I would screw up, thus increasing their chances of a win, or, my team passed it to me knowing that I would mishandle the ball and thus provide more fuel for bullying. I grabbed the ball and began dribbling toward the basket. *I was doing it!* What an amazing feeling. In just the course of a couple of seconds I felt like I was doing something correctly in a team sport. I did not have to go far to make a shot. As I lifted the ball and launched it toward the basket I heard a bellowing voice, "Mabie, you are going the wrong way!" I had headed for, and launched the ball at the opposing team's basket. "Mabie the Baby, you are an idiot," was the next thing I heard. "Get him off our team," was the final comment. I walked to the bench in complete and utter humiliation. The game ended and we headed for the shower room – *dread.*

That day in the shower room was when the towel whipping began. My performance in the basketball game was tremendous fuel for the bullying fire. The results were verbal and physical assaults in the shower, including the sting of a tightly wrapped towel snapped against my legs. The boys were relentless in their attack. I was frozen with fear and could not dream of retaliating. The end of the assault came only when the gym teacher cracked open the door to the shower room and yelled, "Time is up, get back to class."

At the end of that school day the bus came to take us back to the neighborhood. I was numb from the day's events. I remember climbing into the bus in a stupor, barely conscious of my surroundings. There would have to be some major input into my world to make me wake up from my trance. This bus ride provided that input.

As I sat down in my bus seat, there in front of me was the next element that would rock my world. Written on the back of the seat ahead of me, in big bold Magic Marker pen, were the words, *Mabie is Gay*. I was now awake from my stupor. Shock, fear, dread. You see, I did not know what *Gay* really meant, I just knew that it was very bad. There it was in front of me, referencing me. It would be in front of me for the rest of the bus ride. My mind whirled with thought; "Someone was so intent on tormenting me that they were willing to risk their own neck by defacing school property", "Someone hates me so much that they were willing to put it in writing in a place where other school kids would see it", "This will be here for the rest of the school year." My mind and body were so wrapped by fear that I do not remember anything else about that bus ride. I am sure that I was being tormented by others, but I don't remember it.

Seventh grade art class was another adventure. During one particular class, we were assigned the task of *slap* painting. This technique involved slapping the surface of a piece of paper with a paint brush that was laden with paint. The paint would splatter across the paper creating random splashes of color. "Slap, slap, slap," was called out by everyone as the raised brush came crashing down on the piece of paper. I enjoyed this expressive art exercise, until the art teacher excused himself from the classroom for a moment. "I'll be right back," he said. By now, there were two kids that had become the ring leaders with regard to my bullying. More often than not, they were the kids who initiated the various acts against me. Continuing with the *slapping* theme, I was about to enjoy slapping some paint on my paper when instead, I felt the sting of a hand slap on the back of my head. I turned to look and it was one of the ring leaders. Taking advantage of the absence of the teacher, he had initiated his own *slapping* by hitting me against the back of my head. He then exclaimed, "Look at the crap Mabie the Faggot painted!" As if on cue, other kids stood up, approached me from behind and slapped me on the back of my head. It was a procession. They approached en masse, each one taking a turn at slapping me on the back of the head. I sat there as usual, completely frozen by fear. There were just too many of them to even think of taking a stand. I was paralyzed. Slap, slap, slap, slap. The kids heard the steps of the teacher in the hallway as he was returning and they retreated to their desks. I finished the period with a stinging headache and I was unable to paint any longer as a result of the emotional and physical paralysis.

*Faggot*, that was an interesting word that I had not heard before. What did *faggot* mean? I had come to understand, after research in my home encyclopedia, what gay meant and it was a very bad thing. But this faggot word was a mystery. After the art class bell I retreated to the boy's bathroom to relieve myself. I walked into the bathroom stall, turned around and closed the door. It stared me in the face. There, scratched into the paint on the stall door were the words, *CM is Gay*. CM – Craig Mabie. I froze. Just like on the bus seat, someone had taken the time to deface school property in order to make public a very negative reference to me. Then, just below it was scratched, *CM is a Faggot*. I deduced that faggot meant gay. Sitting there on the toilet, I remember intense fear coupled with curiosity. Fear of the public defamation that I was experiencing and curiosity over the gay issue – was I *gay*? Why were they calling me *gay*? Is there something in me that they see that I do not understand or know about? I remember clearly thinking that to be gay is very bad and if I am gay, well, maybe that is what is wrong with me and why I am being subjected to so much torture.

A light bulb went off in my head as I sat on the toilet thinking. Other boys had girlfriends. Why had I never had a girlfriend? Other boys talked about boobs and asses and going around the bases. I never talked of these things, never thought about these things and had no interest in these things. I had never had any interest in or attraction to girls in that way. I had however, noticed boys in a *different* sort of way. Their biceps, faces, physical strength, and hands – all had caught my attention. "*Oh my God – I am gay*," I thought to myself as I sat on that middle school toilet seat. This thought produced in me the greatest sensation of fear that I had felt yet in my life. I remember shaking. The thought did not last long however, and was quickly replaced by denial. I completely dismissed the thought that I might be gay. I told myself that it was just a phase, it's just kid's stuff, I was too young to know, and as I got older I would start to be attracted to girls. I pushed it down, far down, in the hope that it would never surface again.

## Blowing my Horn

As if to be primed for additional insult and injury, I had learned to play the trumpet. This endeavor started in the third grade, before I moved to this current town. The junior high school had a band – barely. The school system that I was in was very team sports centric and placed little value on art or music. It showed in the band. It was small, poorly organized, had little support and was composed mostly of girls. To the kids in school, it was a complete joke. It was the place for sissies, nerds and has-beens. I became a part of it. Not because I wanted to, I did not want to, but because I played the trumpet, my parents, as well as the part time school music teacher, decided that I would join the band. It felt like a death sentence. At that point there was still no amount of pain and suffering that could make me challenge my dad though, so I joined the band.

I had endured much taunting with regard to playing the trumpet and playing in the band. My trumpet case, as I carried it to and from school on the bus, was a big bold proclamation of my status as class loser. "There's the band faggot," was a common exclamation on the bus. It was a great lead in for the continuation of all the types of bullying that I endured. And now it was time for the middle school's annual band concert and I was having forebodings about this event. I experienced my first real breakdown over the anticipation of appearing in this show.

I was in my bedroom preparing for the concert; dressing myself in the dorky uniform, purging the spit from my trumpet and looking over the sheet music. As I prepared, the *dread* grew stronger and stronger. My mind created all kinds of doomsday scenarios. I would screw up the concert by playing the wrong notes, losing my place in the song or missing a cue from the band conductor. But the worse source of *dread*, by far, was the bullying fuel that this concert would provide to all my school adversaries. Mabie the Faggot, Mabie the Loser, CM is Gay – my mind told me that it would all come crashing down on me after my very public band concert display. Sitting in my room, I entered a mental and emotional state that I had not experienced before. I lost control. I was not able to figure a way out, I was not able to manipulate the situation and all I saw was a dead end. I was heading for certain destruction via the band concert.

I got up, walked out into the living room and stood there, shaking and ready to explode from a soup of traumatic emotion that was overpowering, that I did not understand and had not experienced before. My mother entered the living room and saw me standing there. I am sure she saw me shaking. "Are you okay?" she said. I can remember my response clearly. From somewhere deep inside me, for the first time ever, I was about to stand up to and defy my parent's wishes. To do this I first had to defy my mom, a supremely difficult task because I knew that she would go to my dad with the issue and that was the source of the true fear. My mind had always told me that to deny my father meant that I would have to experience his anger, his rejection and ultimately, face my annihilation. Such was the fear that I had of my father. It was a monumental task to respond to my mother; I spoke the following words to her, "I am not going to the band concert." "What? Yes, you are," she said. That response was all it took for me to descend to a place that felt like I was no longer alive, that I was somehow unconscious while standing there, feeling attacked by my mother. My parents were sending me into the hell hole of middle school bullying via the band concert. They, of course, had no idea of how bad things were at school because I had done such a remarkable job of hiding the situation from them. The fear of my father's response, had he known about my situation, was a powerful motivator to keep things under wrap.

I lost it in front of my mother. A full hysterical fit ensued. I cried, I yelled, I pleaded through an intense stream of tears and a thick wall of fears. I can remember the look of shock on my mother's face. I had never behaved in such a manner before; I was always so well behaved. My father walked in. My father.

The air in the room became thicker for me, I had difficulty breathing, and my hysteria deepened. I had clearly lost every shred of self control. I struggled with providing my parents with a reasonable excuse for not participating in the band concert. I had to give them a reason that would be commensurate with the level of drama that I was creating in front of them. Yet, I could not possibly tell them the true reasons for my meltdown. All I could muster was to yell, over and over, "I hate playing the trumpet and I hate playing in the band." This argument, of course, held no water with my father. Despite my breakdown, the tears, pleading, yelling – my hysteria, they told me that I was indeed going to the band concert and that I was going to play in the band. "No, no, no," I shouted, amazing myself that I could stand up to my father. I don't remember what happened next. The next thing that I do remember is being in the car and my parents driving me to the band concert. Strangely, while riding in the back seat on the way to the middle school, I experienced a sense of relief. I had been able to release, through my hysterical breakdown in the living room, in a way that I had never been able to release before. Everything had always remained so bottled up inside me, so stuffed down, that to experience a release of mental and emotional energy in that living room gave me a sense of peace that I had not experienced before. The peace was short lived however, as the middle school came in to view through the car window and I realized that the true source of my hysteria had not been addressed. All the underlying sources of my trauma were there waiting for me, about to be enhanced through a demoralizing and demeaning public viewing.

# Queer Adam
# in the Winter

## Leslie the Faggot

The day after the concert, in the shower after gym class, I heard it for the first time. "Hey, it's Mabie the band geek, just like a lesbian – a lezzy. Hey, it's "Leslie the Faggot," exclaimed one of my bullying ring leaders. Laughter erupted in the locker room at the first utterance of my new moniker. *Leslie the Faggot* were words that would strike a new level of fear and anxiety into my world. Not only was I now being referred to as being gay, but I was being referred to as a gay woman, the meaning of which I came to understand through my own encyclopedia research into the meaning of the word lesbian.

My parents went away for a weekend and decided to hire one of the high school neighborhood girls to stay at our house, overnight, and babysit me. The girl was the older sister of one of the neighborhood boys. As a result, all the neighborhood boys knew that my parents were gone. They knew that I was an open target, and the plot that they executed that Saturday night was deep. The girl and I were in the house, hanging out in the living room and all of a sudden I heard the downstairs door shut. I peered down into the basement to investigate and saw nothing. I went into my bedroom and closed the door, feeling the need for safety. I heard the girl talking to someone, and I froze with terror. Someone else was in the house. Who was in the house? I mustered the courage to leave my room and go talk to the girl who was sitting in the living room. I asked her who was in the house, to whom was she talking to and she replied, "No one, just go into the kitchen and get yourself something to drink." I complied, and as I rounded the corner from the living room to the kitchen, the kitchen coat closet door flung open and out jumped three screaming neighborhood boys. Amongst their screams they shrieked, "Leslie the Faggot needs a babysitter!" Then, from behind me came a physical shove to my body and several other neighborhood boys who were yelling and screaming. They had been hiding in the bathroom and emerged simultaneously with the boys in the closet. I glanced at the girl and saw the smile on her face – she was in on it! I was physically and verbally assaulted from what seemed to be all sides. I was ambushed. Overwhelming fear paralyzed me as I realized what was happening. The safe haven borders of my house had been breached. There was nowhere I could go and nowhere that was safe. The boys continued to run around the house, screaming and yelling, clearly fueled by the success of their surprise attack. I lumbered aimlessly in the kitchen, unable to respond and not having a clue as to what to do. Finally, the girl said, "Okay guys, that's enough, get out of the house." They did not leave. I soon understood that they had no respect for this girl as an authority figure and they were going to play this out as they saw fit. They traveled around the house, inspecting every corner: my bedroom, my parent's bedroom, the family room. I watched in horror as this pack of middle school boys violated every corner of my safe haven. What were they looking at? What were they looking for? What were they taking? How would I explain to my parents if something was missing from the house? Terror. The girl continued to request, with the smile still present on her face, that the boys leave the house. "I could get in trouble," she squealed, as she watched the boys cavort around the rooms. Finally, they left. But I was not sure if all of them had left. They could be hiding in a closet again, ready to pounce on me. I locked each and every door to the house and then methodically inspected every room, every closet and every potential hiding place in the house for an intruder. When I was satisfied that there was no one in the house, I began to calm down. I walked toward my bedroom and saw the girl sitting in the living room. She glanced at me and said nothing. I could not utter a word to her. She had allowed for, even participated in, a complete violation of my world. Knowing that I had to be in her presence for the rest of the evening, overnight and into the next day until my parents returned was terrifying. She was an open door for the neighborhood boys. I walked into my bedroom, closed the door but left it slightly ajar so that I could hear what was going on in the house, and spent the remainder of the evening listening in fear.

Back at school, I went to the bathroom, closed the stall door and saw my new moniker inscribed in the stall door paint, "Leslie the Faggot is Gay," it read. I had almost come to expect it, still, the pain and fear cut deep. I returned to social studies class traumatized and there, waiting for me, was a new adversary. And she had a plan. Clearly fueled by all the bullying that was happening to me, she decided to join in, in her own unique way. She was the seventh grade class's most popular girl. She was tall, pretty, smart, blonde and got the most attention from the boys in the seventh grade. She was seductive and sensual and she knew it. The method she had devised to contribute to my bullying was simple. She would let me know through her words and body language that I would *never* be able to have a girl like her. The teacher excused himself from the social studies class for a moment, left the room and the girl saw her chance. She approached me in my seat, got very physically close to me and said the following directly into my face, looking directly into my eyes. "Leslie the Faggot will never get a girl like me. You see, I am popular, pretty, smart, beautiful and sexy. I am all the things that you will never have or be because you are Leslie the Faggot." The entire class was watching and listening as she continued. "Do you even know what sex is? Of course you don't because you are Leslie the Faggot. What is first base? (I was silent because I did not know) You will never have sex and never be with a girl like me. You are pathetic, no one wants you and…" She heard the teacher's footsteps in the hallway as he headed back toward the classroom. She quickly ended her verbal assault and retreated to her chair, just as the teacher walked in. I sat there stunned as the teacher quickly announced a quiz on some material that we had been learning. I don't remember the content of that quiz; I just remember being unable to concentrate as my mind spun out of control with thoughts of what I had just experienced. I failed the quiz.

## Winter – Glorious, Wonderful Winter!

Ahh, November. Glorious, cold, wet, snowy November! November was the beginning of the winter season in New Hampshire. The onset of cold and snow meant one thing to me – the end of the outdoor team sports season, and some relief. The change of season meant a break from the humiliation that I endured from flag football, kickball and outside gym class. No more team sports trauma, at least for a while. It also meant the start of ski season, and skiing had become a source of salvation in my life. During the winter of the fifth grade, my mother bought me ski lessons at our local hill, at the suggestion of an old boyfriend who owned a ski shop. I had taken to it immediately and over the past two years I had come to understand that I could participate in the sport *alone*. There was no requirement to be part of a team or associate with a group of boys in order to participate in the sport of skiing. I fell in love with it. I loved the snow, the cold, the wind, the sky and the freedom that skiing gave to me.

Come November, I would hole up in my bedroom and obsess over ski magazines while anxiously watching the weather for approaching snowstorms. The thermometer outside my bedroom window became an intimate friend as I watched the temperature drop to that critical, glorious thirty-two degrees Fahrenheit – freezing! This was the start of my lifelong obsession with inclement weather. Inclement November weather meant relief from trauma and the start of skiing.

Skiing became my passion. It was my first taste of actually being good at a sporting activity. I could do it alone, without the omnipresent trauma that I had come to experience; skiing meant relief, peace, and calm – bliss!

But I did not always do it alone. My best friend, the boy I had befriended in sixth grade, was also a skier. Skiing was a powerful connection for us and the experiences we shared on the slopes deepened our friendship. Often, while perched high on the mountain at the top of a ski run, we would take on a unique, challenging and thrilling experience on skis.

It went like this. We would face each other, standing on our skis and oriented perpendicular to the fall line of the slope. Lifting our two ski poles between us and holding them parallel to the ground, I would grab the handle ends of the poles and he would grab the basket ends. Holding tightly, we would turn our skis down the slope and begin to ski straight down the mountain. Once enough velocity was achieved, I would quickly and forcefully initiate a sharp turn which would cause him to whip around me in a circle. The force of the kinetic energy took him below me, and then spun him upslope above me. My body would pivot as he circled so that I was facing directly uphill on my skis as he arced above me. Then he would plunge down the slope next to me, completing the full revolution around my body. This motion would then cause me to whip around him in a similar circular fashion. We repeated these circular whipping motions, becoming one choreographed spinning entity as we proceeded down the slope, all the while gaining forward momentum as well as experiencing increased centrifugal force as we spun faster and faster.

I felt freedom and lightness as we revolved. An energetic thrill rose up in my body and a wide smile stretched across my face. I saw conical slope side evergreen trees and puffy white clouds set in a deep blue winter sky whizzing by me at ever greater speed. I delighted in the expression of pleasure on the face of my best friend, knowing he was experiencing similar sensations.

Then came the aching arms and legs that resulted from the physical exertion necessary to maintain breakneck speed and harness the powerful centrifugal forces. The speed and spinning increased to a point where we could no longer physically withstand the pressures. We reached breaking point, and a hand would release its grip from one of the poles. Our connection severed, the forces would tear us apart and send us careering in opposite directions across the ski slope. Travelling at high speed and completely out of control, we would crash to the ground and skid along the slick snow surface. Skis, poles, hats and goggles detaching from our bodies as we went, finally ending up in a heap on the side of the ski trail.

I came to rest looking up at the beautiful winter sky and laughing. Laughing with a deep, resonant, full body laugh that emanates from an experience of pure joy – a feeling of being fully alive. I looked over at my best friend on the other side of the trail and saw that he was having a similar experience. We caught each other's eye and erupted into further laughter, enjoying our camaraderie as well as the experience that we had created and enjoyed together.

Our skiing adventures were just one part of what became a friendship that was, for me, positive, fun, and affirming. It was a joyous peer association – the opposite of what I was experiencing from so many others at the time. Our skiing escapades provided relief from a different activity that was imposed on me in my youth – shooting.

My father wanted me to be a hunter. Guns and hunting were his passions and he wanted them to be mine as well. When he did pull himself away from the new business, it was to take me hunting. I did not like hunting. I did not like the sound of guns. I could not tell my father this because it would have displeased him, and I had great fear over what his reaction might be. So, I went along with the guns and hunting, even putting on a show as if I was enjoying it. I needed to make sure that I did not ruffle him. Hunting would be an additional source of tension between us that would last for many years. The hardest part was that hunting season corresponded with skiing season. Hunting season in New Hampshire began in earnest in November, just as skiing season was underway. Many a time I found myself in a New Hampshire marsh at the crack of dawn on a cold November morning, trying to spook ducks into flight in order to get off a shot. All the while, wishing I was on the mountain on a pair of skis. At some point and on some level, my father grew to know that skiing was my passion, not guns and hunting. I know that this was difficult for him. I give him credit for spending time with me and for introducing me to the sport that he loved. I also give him credit for eventually supporting my skiing. Although I could not readily access it at the time, deep down I knew that my father loved me and he showed it in the ways that he could. As damaging as his parenting methods could be, he honestly tried and cared.

## Hope?

The two boys that had become the ring leaders for my bullying got chummy with me one day. They invited me over to one of their houses on the next Saturday to "hang out." They invited *me* over? My mind spun over this invitation. Was it a trap? Were they planning some sort of ambush once I got there? They had been very sincere and friendly with their invite. Could it be that this was a window into creating a different relationship with them? Was it an opportunity to stop, or at least reduce the bullying? What if I hung out with them and made a good impression? Maybe they would like me and things would change? I was so desperate for some sort of relief that even the small possibility of change was attractive. From somewhere, I summoned enough courage and made the decision to take them up on their offer and go to the house on Saturday.

This boy's house was actually in a different neighborhood, about a 30 minute walk from my neighborhood. It took some effort to get there. As I approached the house, a gray colored New England colonial, my mind began to fill my head with thoughts – opportunity or ambush? Emotions ensued; trepidation, fear, anxiety, hope. I walked into the yard, up the front door steps and rang the doorbell. One of the two boys answered the door and said, "Hi, come on in." His manner was friendly and open and I felt hope swell up in my body. This hope was a very powerful feeling and one that I had not had much experience with. It felt good. He said, "Have a seat here and wait a minute while I go get the other kid." I sat in a chair in the dining room, filled with anticipation about what we would do.

I was ready to participate fully, put on a great show and make these kids my friends. I would change the way they viewed me and that would change everything. The bullying would stop!

Then I noticed that the house was quiet. The boys had not come back. "It is a big house," I thought to myself, "It will take a while." The silence continued as I sat alone, at the dining room chair. Enough time passed where I began to feel ill at ease. I got up from the chair, walked from the dining room to the kitchen and called the boys' names. No response. Continued silence in the house. Like a titanic ocean wave, fear rolled over my body. Something was wrong. I proceeded to walk around the rooms of the house, calling the boys' names. I received no response. My mind was busy creating all kinds of scenarios; they were hiding on me, they were going to jump out of a closet and scare me, they were going to do *something* to me, but what? And then came the thought that nearly paralyzed me with fear, had they trapped me in the house? Were the doors locked so I could not escape? An enormous surge of energy welled inside me that drove me to flee with all the speed I could muster. I ran as fast as I could toward the front door, terrified that I would be met with a locked, impenetrable barrier. The door opened and I catapulted my body down the steps and out onto the lawn. As I was running away from the house I heard it, "Leslie the Faggot is a baby and has no friends!" I turned around to look and there were the two boys, hanging out of a window of the house, taunting me. They had been in the house all along, hiding from me. They had worked out and executed a diabolical plan, and it had worked. They duped me into thinking that I could become their friend. They had invited me to the house with the full intention of hiding from me and making my trip to this neighborhood a waste of time. They played me – successfully. As I walked home, tears rolling down my face, I thought of what school would be like on Monday once all the kids learned of my newest humiliation.

## Dumb

The summer between seventh and eighth grade arrived – finally. Once again, the summer brought tremendous relief. I activated all my finely honed strategies for avoiding the neighborhood boys. I explored the woods and attained some peace. It was all good until, toward the end of August, the *dread* of the new school year crept in.

The eighth grade brought with it French class – a new learning opportunity. I liked the language; something about it resonated with me. I was able to quickly master the accent, learn the vocabulary and speak with confidence. I was good at it! This was a new feeling for me. The entirety of the trauma that I had experienced in the last several years of school had dramatically affected my academic performance. It was all I could do to muster enough mental energy to just complete my school work, forget about doing or learning it well. Then came this French, and I was good at learning it and speaking it. In the class I was a star and the teacher recognized it. She gave me accolades during the class and I began to stand out. The boys could not handle this. For the last several years my position in the social hierarchy of the school was at the very bottom. They were not used to seeing me excel or be lifted up. They did not like it and chose to take action against it. There came a time in French class when we had to choose a name for ourselves. I had always liked the name Adam so I decided to choose this name as my French name. The teacher went around the room asking each kid to state their new name in English and then she would say it in French. She got to me and I said that I wanted my name to be Adam. She then pronounced the name in French, "Adum." There was laughter from the class and the bullies pounced. They saw their opportunity to cut me down to my normal, bottom of the barrel social status. From then on I was referred to as *A-dumb* and was told that I had picked the perfect name to represent myself – *dumb*. The light of French class had dimmed.

# Out and About?

## White Hoods

It was a January Saturday evening during an eighth grade winter night – dark, deep and cold. I was in the basement watching TV and listening to the neighborhood boys playing outside in the snow.

My parents had gone out to dinner and the neighbor girl was once again babysitting me. This time I had been smart. I made sure that all the doors and windows to the house were locked so that the boys could not get in. I had not anticipated another potential threat, however.

I heard a knock on the front door. I ran upstairs, dashed to the living room and toward the front door. I saw my babysitter standing at the door, with it about half way open as she said, "Hello." Before she knew it, the door was pushed fully open by the neighborhood boys on the other side and into the house five of them came. I felt the familiar sensation of terror radiating from my stomach into all parts of my body. Another violation of my space, my life, my sanctuary was occurring. They found my father's liquor cabinet and began to drink from the bottles. I was terrified! My father would know that some of his liquor was missing and question me about it. My mind went into overdrive. What would I tell him? Would I say that a hoard of marauding neighborhood boys came into the house and consumed the liquor? I could not say that as he would condemn me for not standing up to them and defending the house. He might find out about all the bullying and condemn me to a life of shame for being a *Sissy*. He would find out that I was *Gay*, that I was **Leslie the Faggot**. It was unthinkable. Would I tell him that I drank it? I could not do that. My annihilation would be complete as I would be subject to his wrath and the frightful beating via the wooden spoon.

The herd of boys running through the kitchen awoke me from the torturous thoughts that were playing out in my mind. I heard the babysitter yell, "Quick, get out, the Mabies are coming home!" The sound of the garage door opener activating and lifting the garage door was heard in the house – my parents were returning from their evening. The boys made an about face and headed for the back door of the house. They fled out the door, into the backyard and the cold January night. I rushed to arrange the bottles in the liquor cabinet back to their original positions, as best as I could remember, and closed the liquor cabinet door. The babysitter was working fast to return the house to a respectable condition. I turned on the basement TV, flung myself onto the couch and pretended that the evening had been as normal and mundane as possible, as my parents walked in.

I remained glued to the couch as my parents settled down for the rest of their evening. I stared at the TV, but nothing from the program was registering. I was in a daze of constant and continuous mind thought as I relived the events of the evening and constructed all the potential scenarios regarding the missing liquor. I kept a keen ear, searching for the sounds of my father opening the liquor cabinet in order to make himself a drink. I was on edge and terrified.

Like a shot ringing in the dark night, my mother's raised voice suddenly permeated every corner of the house. "What is that? Come here, quick, look outside," she yelled to my father in a high pitched, nervous and shrill voice. My mother never raised her voice. Her vocal reaction to whatever was going on outside was alarming. Lying there on the couch, my current state of terror was infused with curiosity. I launched myself toward and up the stairs, entered the kitchen and then the living room. There, standing at the living room window and looking out at the snow covered front lawn were both of my parents. Their mouths were open with astonishment. I ran to the bathroom window to get the same view of the front lawn, when the signature event of my young life materialized in front of me. There on the front lawn, planted firmly in the snow and right next to a tree, was a wooden cross that was ablaze. My mind reeled as the full force of what I was observing hit me. The neighborhood boys had constructed a wooden cross and set it on fire on my front lawn. A fucking burning cross was on my front lawn! I stood there at the bathroom window, incapacitated by fear, when I heard my father spring into action. He grabbed a coat from the hall closet and barreled down the front steps in the house, burst through the front door and catapulted his body out into the deep snow of the front lawn. He picked up snow with his bare hands and threw it at the burning cross until the flames were extinguished. Once the fire was out, he kicked the base of the cross with his boot until the cross fell down into the snow. He tromped on the cross numerous times, driving it further into the snow to make sure that it was extinguished and to cool the wood. He paused and looked at the smoking cross lying there half buried in the snow. My mind thought about what his mind must be thinking. Did he know who did it, as I did? Did he have a clue how relentless and cruel the neighborhood boys could be? Did he think they were capable of this – a prank that had the potential to set fire to a house? Did he think it was someone else? My family, and especially my father, had exhibited deep prejudice against Blacks throughout my life; did he think it was a Black person seeking revenge on him? I had come to learn that my father exhibited some rather unethical business practices at the business that he owned. Did he think that it was some work associate that was exacting revenge? I knew, based on experiencing prejudice that ran deep in my family, that the Ku Klux Klan burned wooden crosses to incite fear in their adversaries. Did my father think that the Klan was targeting us? He must have wondered why because we were not Black or Jewish. "What would he do?" I wondered as I watched him pick up the extinguished and charred cross, walk to the driveway, put it down and then disappear into the night. My mind was spinning with terror and for some reason it settled on the white hooded Ku Klux Klan. What exactly was it? I ran to my room and opened up my encyclopedia to look up the Klan. I read the words anti-Black, anti-Jewish, anti-Catholic, anti-Communist, and then I froze as I read the words – anti-Homosexual. CM is Gay. Mabie the

Faggot. Leslie the Faggot. The boys had burned a cross on our lawn to mimic the action of the Ku Klux Klan in reference to the organization's stance regarding gay people. In reference to *me*! I sat on the floor of my room trembling with angst. Did my father think it was the neighborhood boys and was he going after them? If he did, would they say something with regard to *my gayness* and tip my father off to the issue? The tremendous fear of the burning cross on the front lawn was instantaneously replaced with the even greater fear of my father thinking I was gay.

I swallowed hard to keep from vomiting, closed the encyclopedia and propped myself against the side of my bed. I sat there in a cloud of thought and emotion that was so deep and complex that I lost track of time. I do not know how long I sat there, immobilized, but I know that it was a significant period. I was jolted out of my stupor some time later by the sound of the outside door opening and slamming shut. My father had returned. What was to happen next? What had he found out in the night? What had he done? I was filled with so much dread that all I could think to do was to shut my bedroom door, take off my clothes, turn off the light, crawl into my bed and pretend to fall asleep. Eventually my mother came to check on me. She opened the door to my room, observed that I appeared to be asleep and then shut the door. I laid there awake for hours, anticipating what I would experience at school on Monday, once the neighborhood boys had spread the word of the burning cross. That paled in comparison to my thoughts of the questions that my dad would ask me the next morning. None of it was as traumatic as the image of the burning cross that was seared into my mind.

I sat at the breakfast table the next morning, tired and red-eyed from the lack of sleep. I nervously waited for my parents to start a conversation about the burning cross; to ask me questions about the hate symbol that had appeared on our front lawn the night before. And yet, no questions came; not a word about it was spoken. I sensed the opportunity to escape without interrogation, and so I quickly finished my breakfast and departed for school. The burning cross was never mentioned. My parents had obviously made the decision, for reasons that I did not understand and did not care to understand, that it was a topic that would not be discussed with me. It was a tremendous relief.

## Yes I Am. No I'm Not.

The gymnasium at the middle school doubled as the lunch room. Tables and benches would fall down from out of the wall, just like a Murphy bed, and all of us seventh and eighth graders would sit down and eat lunch in the cavernous gym. Lunch was always consumed in less time than the actual lunch period, and in the remaining time a daily arm wrestling contest had materialized. I enjoyed this arm wrestling contest, which was very unusual as I had come to abhor competition of any kind. The boys would roll up the long sleeves of their shirt, or push their short sleeves up on their shoulder, to get ready for the arm wrestle. There were several boys that had well developed, muscular arms, and I enjoyed looking at them. At one lunch period in particular, I can remember looking at a couple of the boys and thinking they were handsome. I remember feeling sexually attracted to them. Then came the unbridled fear as I realized what I was thinking and feeling. Leslie the Faggot! The kids were right, I was gay! How did they know before I did? As I sat there thinking about it, watching their muscular arms tense with the engagement of the arm wrestle, I recognized that this was far from the first time that I had looked at boys and felt sexual attraction.

The attraction was so strong that I actually mustered the courage to challenge one of the boys that I found attractive to an arm wrestle. It was a defining moment for me. He accepted the challenge, we sat across from one another and he raised his forearm and hand into the challenge position. I remember sensing an excitement within me that I had never sensed before as I visually scanned his hand and arm. I reached out to form the same challenge position and clasped his hand. It was electric. The touch, the feel, the warmth of his hand was like nothing I had ever felt before. "Ready, set, go!" he exclaimed. Suddenly, I felt the pressure and the power of his gripping hand and flexing arm. I saw the slight grimace on his face as he summoned his strength. I responded with all the strength I had. It was exhilarating to feel the strength come forth from my body and create an opposing force to his. I was on fire. It was undeniable – I was having my first experience of full-on adolescent sexual attraction. He was infinitely stronger than I was and very quickly I felt my arm give way to a tremendous force and crash onto the lunch table with a thud. "Leslie the Faggot," he exclaimed, knowing that that was all he had to say to make his point. "Next," he shouted as he summoned his next arm wrestling challenger.

I retreated into the obscurity of the lunchroom with my

mind awhirl. I had a full and complete understanding that I had just experienced intense sexual attraction toward this boy and it was absolutely terrifying. My emotions were in overdrive; shame, guilt and fear were overtaking me. A powerful defense mechanism, one that had been created before and was now familiar, became activated. Repress it, stuff it, and bury it deep inside. It is a phase that will go away. Soon you will have the same attraction with girls; you just are not old enough yet. This attraction to boys will pass. Get a girlfriend. Yea, that's it! I need a girlfriend to activate these same sensations with girls. The lunch period bell rang and it was time to head back to eighth grade class. As I walked down the hall toward the classroom I was trying to think of any girls that would want to be my girlfriend. None came to my head as my mind told me that no girl would want to be the girlfriend of the school loser.

I had noticed her in the eighth grade home room period. She was a girl whom I had watched become relegated to *loser* status by the other eighth grade girls. She was a little dowdy, frumpy, and overweight and had an acne problem. She was clearly unpopular, just like me. "Ah hah!" I said to myself, "She might be a girl who would be interested in having me as a boyfriend." I can remember my mind playing out all kinds of scenarios. I would make her my girlfriend and in so doing I would become attracted to a girl for the first time. I would come to understand what all the other eighth grade boys were talking about as they expressed their desire to *round the bases* with girls, or grab their boobs and asses, or have this thing called *sex* with them. I would come to know all these things that I had not experienced or understood about attraction to the female sex, but had witnessed in so many of the other boys as they related to girls.

I became friendly toward her. I went out of my way to engage her and interact with her. I made her my focus. She recognized all of this and she responded in kind. There was a school dance class and I asked her to be my dance partner. I was *determined* to get close enough to her so that the male/female attraction would kick in. I did all of this with great purpose, and I waited. I waited for the excitement, the feelings and the sexual energy to appear. It never did. It turned out to be an exercise in frustration as no sexual attraction or sexual feelings ever arose. And yet, the minute the lunch room arm wrestling began with the boys, all of those sexual feelings rushed over me. It was undeniable.

Yet, it became my sole mission to deny those feelings. I became a master at stuffing the feelings of attraction toward boys. I felt that certain obliteration would come to me if I did not. I also stopped trying with the girl, or with any girl, as my attempt to raise sexual attraction with the girl was a resounding failure. When I withheld the attention that I had been giving her, she was hurt or insulted in some way and she lashed out at me. She picked up the well known themes of *CM is Gay*, and *Leslie the Faggot*, adding her voice to the chorus of gay insults that I was receiving from other classmates. She added to the defamation by telling as many classmates as she could that, "He likes his *trumpet* more than he likes me." This was a clear reference to my loser status as a trumpet player in the school band and added more fuel to the bullying fire that was burning so strongly under me.

## Unconscious RAGE

It was springtime and near the end of the eighth grade school year. The bullying, in all its various forms, had continued throughout the year in unrelenting fashion. And so it was that I found myself sitting in a science class listening to the teacher lecture. As I sat there I noticed that a note was being secretly passed between my classmates. Whenever the teacher turned her back to the class in order to write on the chalkboard, the note would be passed. I saw that the note had ended up with one of the two bullying ringleaders. This kid had been responsible for much of the bullying that I had experienced over the last four years of my life. The note made me very nervous. Many times over the past four years, notes had been passed around by and to my classmates that contained very derogatory comments about me. It was a bullying technique that had been in frequent use. I knew that chances were good that this particular note, on this particular day, was about me and that it was saying something hurtful. I noticed, as each kid got the note and read it, that a smirk came over their face and they glanced at me. That confirmed it; the note was about me – again. In addition to smirking and glancing my way, I also noticed that each kid wrote something on the note and that was a tactic I had not seen before. The note came to rest with the primary instigator and, when the teacher turned her back once again, he slipped the note onto my desk. The note had been folded to conceal the text that was inside, but, on the outside of the note, clearly visible, were the words, *You better open this now and read this. You're dead after school tonight.* I was horrified. For the first time in four years of bullying a threat had actually been made on my life. You see, the bullying had been so intense, so deep and so powerful for so long that I actually believed that these kids could and would kill me if given the right chance. I sat there, looking at the words and felt a primal fear well up inside me. I realized that some of these kids had actually become big and strong enough to do me a great deal of physical harm – even kill me.

I looked at the perpetrator. He pointed his finger at me and mouthed the words, "You are *dead*." I felt eyes glancing at me from around the room. The teacher lectured throughout all of this, but her words were a muddled mess of sound. My brain could simply not process anything other than the myriad of thoughts that were going around in my head about what was to happen to me after school. My body could do nothing but sit there motionless, paralyzed by the intensity of the emotions that were swirling through the tissues of my body.

When the teacher's back was turned once again, I managed to open the note. It read, *Leslie the Faggot deserves to die and will be beat to death after school today.* Below this text were the signatures of everyone that the note had been passed to in the class prior to the note being given to me. There were *many* signatures.

There in my chair, I experienced the deepest level of dread, fear and anxiety that I had yet to experience in my young life. Then, I reached some other place. I entered a world that was foreign to me. The classroom no longer existed in my awareness. Nothing existed in my awareness, except for one, new, startling piece of energy. *Rage.* It welled up inside me as a new force, emanating from some place far beyond my understanding and far beyond my ability to control. It grew to consume me as I sat in my chair. The feeling was complete and overwhelming. I was not conscious; I was unconscious – completely enveloped in and permeated by this new, consuming rage energy. My tormentor tapped on his desk to get my attention and once again mouthed the words, "You are *dead*."

The rage exploded inside me. With a power that I had never experienced and in the blink of an eye, the rage activated every muscle in my body. Like a torpedo I launched at my tormentor from my chair. Right there, in the middle of eighth grade science class while the teacher was lecturing, I physically attacked him. *Me* – the meek, withdrawn, docile, physically incapable and diminutive kid was physically assaulting another boy. My hand clenched into a fist and from some unknown place, the ability to throw a punch materialized. My full-blown, rage-energized punch, landed square on his face. I heard my knuckles crack on his nose. The blood shot forth, hitting me in the face. I felt completely unconscious; unaware of what I was doing, my surroundings and what was taking place. All that I can remember was *rage*. All consuming *rage*. Instantaneously my arm coiled back and then thrust forward once again. Another crack from my knuckles impacting his nose. The blood that was now pouring from his nostrils spurted forth once again and splattered my face. The *rage* flowed. It was an unstoppable force that carried me along like a rapid wild river. My arm coiled back again and I struck once more. A third direct hit to the nose.

As my arm pulled back to prepare for the fourth blow,

something pulled me back to consciousness. I felt a sharp, searingly painful blow to my ribcage. My attack had gone on long enough now for one of the other boys to see what was going on and to react. He had punched me, hard, in the ribcage. He was defending my tormentor and trying to strike me down. I caught a glimpse of his face – it was determined and hateful. I then felt another blow to my abdomen, from another boy, and I recoiled in pain. My mind was somehow once again able to produce thought, and I realized that the other boys in the class were coming to the rescue of my tormentor. They were attacking me. My mind instantly flashed to the death threat in the note. It was happening. This was it. It was not going to wait until after school, as the note had said, it was happening now. Four years of constant torment were coming to a head. My mind quickly realized what I had done to my tormentor; it was the catalyst that was needed to give the boys the permission that they needed to kill me. They would claim self defense. I felt fear beginning to replace rage. The rage energy in my body flowed out and away from me, and I was no longer able to produce muscular action. The rage was replaced by the old and familiar state of being frozen by fear. I awaited my extermination.

The classroom was jolted by the sharp and elevated voice of the teacher. She had heard the sounds of the attack, turned around and saw what was going on. "Stop that right now," she yelled as she thrust her body toward the fight. I felt her strong presence coming in from the right. She was a tall, large boned woman with a commanding physical presence. "Stop it, get back in your seats," she screamed as her hand came crashing down on my shoulder. "Mabie did it," came from a voice in the room. "Mabie attacked him, it is Mabie's fault," came from another voice in the room. "Yea, it was Mabie," was yelled from many kids joining in the chorus of my accusation. Fingers were pointed at me from all points of the room. "Sit down and nobody move," the teacher exclaimed as she rushed to grab some tissues from a nearby counter. She placed the tissues on my perpetrator's nose to stop the bleeding, gently grabbed him by the arm and said, "Come on now, we are going to the nurse's office." She then grabbed my arm, with a force and grip that sent a message that I was in serious trouble. She looked at me and said with a very stern voice, "Come with me, young man, you are going to the principal's office." We quickly departed the classroom to the sound of voices exclaiming, "Mabie did it!"

We moved quickly and entered the nurse's office. The teacher told me, in a very firm voice, "Sit down and stay there." I complied and she disappeared into the office while I sat in the waiting room. As I sat there I could feel my heart racing. My body was electric and alive from what had just transpired, from what I had done. The teacher emerged, grabbed me by the arm once again and said, "You are coming with me to the principal's office." We entered his office with purpose and, sensing our presence and the change of energy in the room, he whirled around in his desk chair. The teacher sat me down in a chair that was on the other side of his mammoth desk. She sat in a chair right next to me and exhaled loudly. It then hit me that I was in the principal's office because I was in trouble. Well mannered, quiet, perfectly behaved *me*, was sitting across from the principal because I was in trouble! It was inconceivable. Never had I imagined myself to be in this place and in this position. He appeared huge on the other side of the desk. He had big hair and massive sideburns and was dressed in a dark, very conservative suit. He was looking right at me as he asked, "Well, what is going on here?" The teacher then explained to him what had happened. I listened as she recounted the attack in great detail. It was amazing to hear the words that described what I had done. It did not feel real, and yet I knew that it was real. I knew that I had done exactly what she described to the principal. She finished her description of the event and then stopped talking. There was silence in the office. For what seemed like an eternity, the principal said nothing. My mind flew into action. "He is going to punish me in some humiliating way," I thought to myself. "He is going to take some disciplinary action that will be public, like making me apologize to the perpetrator in front of my classmates," I fretted. This would be fodder for the kids to initiate a new round of bullying. My mind whirled and my emotions roared. I broke down into tears as I sat in that chair. Sobbing, crying and desperate, I awaited my fate from the principal. The silence was finally broken by the principal's voice as he yelled to his secretary in the other room. "Get me Mrs. Mabie's phone number please."

He was going to call my mother. This eventuality had not yet crossed my mind. My parents would find out what I had done. As a shot of terror released in my gut at this realization, my desperate crying intensified. My father would kill me. He would find out about all the bullying, about his gay son, *Leslie the Faggot*, and I would be annihilated. All of the monumental effort that I had put in to hiding the bullying from him would be wasted. For four long years I had successfully hidden my trauma from him, but now, it was to be revealed in all its ugliness. Mabie the Baby, Mabie the Sissy, Mabie the Loser, CM is Gay, Leslie the Faggot – all of it would be revealed. This was the end result that was far worse than anything I had endured at school or at the hands of the neighborhood boys. The principal called my house, my mother answered and after the standard pleasantries the principal said, "Mrs. Mabie, your son has been in a fight at school and he needs to go home for the rest of the day. Can you please come pick him up?" I heard muffled, indecipherable, anxious words coming from the phone as my mother's voice elevated. Then everything went blank. The level of emotion and mind thought I was experiencing must have become too great for me to handle, and I descended into a place of deep sobbing that blocked out everything else. I do not remember another thing until my mother arrived at the school.

I had been placed in a chair outside the principal's office to wait for her. I saw her walking down the hallway toward me, quickness in her step that was foreign to me. She approached me with the care and concern that she had always showed me and asked if I was okay. I do not remember my response, but I do remember hearing the voice of the secretary, "Mrs. Mabie, the principal would like to see you." My mother disappeared into his office. My mind was replaying, over and over at lightning speed, the scene that the principal was now describing to my mother. Of how I had physically attacked a boy in the middle of eighth grade science class. I imagined the forms of discipline that he might be suggesting to her. Of what he thought my *father* should do to me as an appropriate punishment. I knew what my father's punishment would be. Since I was so afraid of my father, I had rarely gotten in trouble that warranted his punishment. But, it had happened once or twice and it went like this:

My father would call me to the kitchen where he would be sitting in his chair at the kitchen table. He would tell me to walk over to the utensil drawer, pull out the long handled wooden cooking spoon and bring it to him. I would comply and as I handed it to him he would say, "Now turn around in front of me and take your pants down." Knowing what was to come, it was an impossibly difficult thing to do. I can remember his voice, "Take your pants down *now*. For every second you delay, you will get an additional beating with the wooden spoon." The intensity of the fear that was streaming through my body – a combination of a deep, innate fear of my dad and the fear of bodily harm and pain – created a partial physical paralysis that caused me to delay, thus increasing the severity of the beating.

"Now bend over," I would hear him say. The sound of the *crack* of the wooden spoon landing on the soft tissue of my ass was always the first jolt. Then came the searing, all body pain as the shock wave of my father's powerful stroke landing on my bare buttocks reverberated throughout my body. I can remember my face constricting into a tightness that brought tears to my eyes as my body recoiled against the blow. My father's powerful hand, holding me in place at my shoulder, gripped hard as he prepared for the next blow. *Crack* went the wooden spoon as it hit my ass on flesh that was now much more tender as a result of the first blow. My pain increased, as did the tears, humiliation and anger. Several more blows would occur. I can remember the intense longing that each blow would be the last. *Crack* would jolt me back into reality and the realization that he was not done. He did not yet feel that the beating was sufficient punishment and so on it would go. When finally he judged that the punishment had fit the crime he would exclaim, "Now, pull up your pants and go to your room and stay there." As I brought my pants to my waist the friction of the fabric against my pummeled ass would bring a new round of pain. I remember walking to my room, employing an awkward gait that would help to minimize that pain that I was experiencing on my backside. There in my room, I would try to find a way to relax and get comfortable, which was difficult because I could not sit without a great deal of pain.

In my room, my mind developed what, for many years to come, would be one of the signature dysfunctions of my life. My thoughts and emotions created an intense and powerful anger toward my father. My mind then created a fantasy where great harm would come to me – death – as a result of the punishment that my father had just inflicted on me. He would be filled with remorse and sorrow over the fact that he had killed me. This would punish him; make him *pay* for what he had done to me. In this fantasy I took great satisfaction and pleasure in watching him suffer over the loss of his child. The loss that he caused. I would sit in my room and stew for hours, incorporating the combination of the intense anger toward my father and the *make him pay* death fantasy. It created an imprint on my young psyche that would haunt me for years to come. As subsequent years arrived and whenever life did not go well for me, this imprint would activate. My mind would travel to the fantasy: "I am now dead because of what he or she did to me. You killed me because of your cruelty. Now you will pay with your remorse and sorrow. You will see, in my death, just how great a person I was and what a mistake you have made by killing me." I loved the attention that would be lavished on me in this fantasy. This would be coupled with the intense anger that was part of the imprint. It was a soup of dysfunctional fantasy, mind thought and emotion that would completely overtake me, time and time again, whenever life presented a situation which was difficult, unpleasant, frightening or threatening.

The fantasy took on another form as well. I can remember conjuring intense ill will toward my father and seeking control over him. This transformed into the need for control in my life, and control made me feel good. It was a sense of pleasure for me to be in control and therefore be superior in some way. I had so little control and felt so inferior in so many aspects of my life, that to feel like I was *better than* someone was intoxicating. This fantasy created the following imprint on my psyche. If something was wrong in another person's life, if they made a mistake or experienced misfortune, I felt built up in comparison. I felt superior and in control. I found myself getting a high from other people's suffering. I found myself wishing for and hoping for suffering in others so I could create a *high* in myself. It was an invigorating feeling and I craved it. In a strange twist, this transformed into the desire to help others. I could exercise, incorporate and use my "superior" position to assist another person. It was a powerful motivator for me and I would seek out people in distress and assist them in order to make myself feel better.

My mother emerged from the principal's office, grabbed my hand and said in a soft voice, "Come with me and let's go home." I felt a tremble in her hand as we walked down the hallway and out the door. Once in the car, my mother asked me, "So, what happened?" I hesitated as my mind grappled with what I was about to say. With a catch in my throat I replied, "I punched a kid in the face." "Why did you do that?" she asked. My mind quickly reverted to all the well honed strategies that I had developed over the past five years to hide the bullying from my parents. I realized that I still had some control, and I could perhaps minimize the amount of information I would relinquish about this situation. I could minimize the possibility that my father would discover Mabie the Baby, Mabie the Sissy, Mabie the Loser, CM is Gay and Leslie the Faggot. With lightning speed my mind formulated a response that called upon the wealth of deception tactics that had served me so well over the years, and I replied with a resounding, "I don't know."

"What do you mean, 'I don't know'," she said. "Did he do something to you?" In a flash I replied, "He was teasing me." What a perfect response, I thought to myself. Teasing – such a mundane action. For me, it conjured the image of provocation, but nothing too serious. Certainly nothing like a death theat. It would be a reason for me to take action against someone, but nothing that would set off major alarm bells. And then it dawned on me, just how brilliant this response had been. The thought entered my mind that my father was the type of man who would actually be *proud* of me for punching another boy in the face. He would see my act of aggression as manly, macho, strong and aggressive. "That's my boy!" I could hear him exclaim. It would be the exact opposite of Mabie the Baby, Mabie the Sissy, Mabie the Loser, CM is Gay, Leslie the Faggot. I would avoid my annihilation. I might even get some praise! My mother said, "Well, we will talk about it with your father tonight." I felt an enormous sense of relief fall across my emotionally and mentally battered psyche, coupled with a rising fear as my mind played with the alternative possibility that I could be wrong and that I would feel the disciplinary wrath of my father.

That evening, I was sitting on the couch in the basement watching TV when I heard the front door open and slam close. My father was home from work. Now was the time. I listened intently as the two of them had conversation up in the kitchen. I could not make out the words, but I knew the topic was about my behavior at school and the events of the day. A toxic combination of curiosity, anxiousness, excitement, fear and impatience caused me to feel ill in my stomach. When would the dreaded words emanate from the kitchen? – "Craig, come here please." I listened intently, waiting for the call. But it did not come as I had planned. Time dragged on, *The Price Is Right* finished on the TV and the local news program began. I watched the news, and still I had not been summoned to the kitchen. Finally, my mother's words cut through the anxious air of my basement world and I heard, "Craig, come up for dinner please." How odd. Her words and voice were not laden with any sign of impending doom. It was a very normal, everyday type of summoning to the dinner table.

I found that it was very hard to get up from the couch. My body was so heavy with mental and emotional energy that my muscles were slow to respond. I plodded up the basement stairs, emerged into the kitchen and came face to face with my father. "Hi Henry," my father said (my nickname was Henry; he rarely called me by my birth name). He had a look on his face that was not angry, harsh or aggressive – it was bordering on pleasant. In that moment I knew. At the deepest core of my being I knew. My father had taken the path of being proud of me for punching the kid in the face. I was about to learn just how delighted he was. The next words out of his mouth were, "After dinner I am going to take you to the bike store to buy you a new bike for punching that kid in the face." It felt like a raging rapid river of water, laden with thought and emotion, was draining out of my body. In an instant, I could breathe again. In an instant I felt hope. I had succeeded. Leslie the Faggot, and all that it represented, would remain hidden from view. We finished dinner and headed to the bike store.

After the purchase of the new bike was complete and we were back at home it hit me. What type of retaliation would I face the next morning on the bus and at school? The monumental events of the day would have ramifications with my middle school peers, this I knew for certain. But what would happen, what would they do? I got into bed that night filled with angst over the uncertainty of what was to come next. Would they kill me tomorrow, like they had threatened? Then an idea occurred to me. An idea that before this day would have been so foreign, so unthinkable, and yet here it was, suddenly consuming me. I could fight back again! I could punch again. I could inflict bodily harm again. It was a rush of power that I had never experienced. I imagined striking a blow to the second of my two middle school bullying perpetrators. *It felt so good* to play it out in my mind. But then, I suddenly remembered that two other boys had struck me in the classroom that day. The only reason that they stopped, I surmised, was because the teacher interrupted and broke up the fight. What if they attacked me when the teacher was not around? Like after school, or at the bus stop or on the walk home from the bus stop? What if there was a group of them, like there so often was, and there was nothing to stop all of them from beating me to a pulp? My mind whirled and my emotions flared. There was no way that I could fight back with any effectiveness against the pack of boys. There were just too many of them. I realized that this group attack was the likely scenario. I also realized that my bed sheets were wet from the drench of sweat that my body was producing from the anxiety, as I lay there, in complete emotional agony.

I went to school the next morning. It was one of the last days of the eighth grade school year and I realized that if I made it through the day, that summer, glorious anxiety-reducing summer would soon be at hand. I made sure that I walked to the bus stop as late as possible so that I could avoid the neighborhood pack of boys as they walked to the school bus. As I had worked out and been able to do so many times, I caught a different bus than the one that the boys were on. Hurdle number one for the day had been passed. I arrived at school and hesitantly entered the middle school building. I remember being acutely aware of my surroundings; on constant guard for an attack. With hyper vigilance I proceeded through the day, making sure to have as little eye contact and interaction with my peers as possible. I wanted to do *nothing* that could possibly provoke an assault. I remember feeling intense fear as, for the first time that day, I saw the victim of my attack. I could not help myself – I had to look at him. His nose was bandaged and he had deep, dark, black and blue marks radiating from his nose and enveloping his eyes. It was at that point that I understood just how hard and how many times I had punched him.

His eyes met mine and he immediately glanced down. He glanced *down* and turned away, and that was something new. He was not aggressive with word and action toward me, as he had always been. We entered the classroom and I knew that something had changed. The Social Studies class ended and my perpetrator came up to me and said, "Hey, how ya doin?" I said, "Fine," as he walked out the door toward the next class of the day. I walked down the hallway in bewilderment. He had addressed *me* with a pleasantry that was not laced with the aggression of bullying. Something had definitely changed. The school day moved through to completion and I was not attacked. I rode the late bus home, as usual, to avoid the ride and walk home with the neighborhood boys. Arriving at the house, I plunged into the safety of the basement, turned on the TV and escaped into the safety of my refuge.

# Lost

## The Complex

Looking back, I can now see that I left the eighth grade with a seriously damaging mental and emotional complex in place. The physical, mental and emotional assaults that I had endured over the four years from fourth to eighth grade, coupled with the fears of my father, had left me with deep wounds of insecurity, low self-esteem, loneliness, feeling like I was not good enough and unfathomable fears and questions regarding my sexuality. I shall refer to this intricate soup of mind and emotion as my *Complex*. It was from this place that I embarked on my next life journey.

## New Wave

The summer was glorious. My parents rented a cottage on a lake in New Hampshire for the month of July. My best friend came along for the month and we went on adventure after adventure, day after day – it was liberating. The lake was a place for me to be completely free from the neighborhood, school and my peers – free from the trauma of bullying and the fears and uncertainty of homosexuality. It also showed me that I was capable of creating a wonderful friendship with another boy – a peer. This was something that had been elusive for me during the last four years. My best friend and I created a lifetime of healthy experiences and memories during that time at the cottage. I will be forever grateful to him for the gift of his friendship that summer and to my parents for giving me the gift of the time at the lake.

August came and the familiar dread of a new school year set in. This time however, it was quite a bit different. I was moving from the middle school in my small town, to attend my freshman year at a high school in a much larger town. Twenty times larger. This new town was more of a city – one of the largest in New Hampshire. The high school was enormous compared to the very small elementary and middle schools that I had attended. My eighth grade class graduated with about thirty-five students and my freshman class would contain 700 students. All the neighborhood boys and most of my peers from the eighth grade would be attending this high school as well.

The change of school created a great deal of anxiety in me. I was scared about the prospect of the continuation of all the bullying at this new school as my eighth grade peers spread the word of who I was and what I was about – as they inevitably would. The fear was compounded by all the unknowns associated with this new world that I was about to enter. And then there was the bus ride to the high school which was three times as long as it had been to the middle school. That was an enormous amount of time for the neighborhood boys and my eighth grade peers to work their bullying tactics – I was petrified of the new bus ride.

And so it was that I found myself, once again, full of angst as the new school year arrived. Then a savior appeared in the form of one of the neighborhood parents. She suggested that the neighborhood form a carpool to take us kids to and from the high school. This would save a lot of time at the beginning and the end of the day as a car ride would be much quicker than the bus. Most of the neighborhood parents signed on to the idea and the carpool was born. No bus ride meant no bullying for me – a few kids in a car with a parent so close was not the right environment. As my parents told me that the carpool was the plan, I remember the enormous sense of relief that came over me. At least my rides to and from school would be free from trauma.

The high school was liberating! There were so many kids, so much more diversity and so much more activity that it was relatively easy to stay away from my small town peers and neighborhood boys. I found people that were more like me and I made friends. I found great joy in making friends at school. Finding peers that would not taunt or hassle me, but rather befriend me, was an amazing experience. I blossomed. I found strength and vitality that had been mostly missing from my small town school experience. I got involved, not with team sports of course because they still struck fear in my heart, but with academic and social pursuits. I joined the group that was creating and sponsoring a *New Wave Dance* at the school. New Wave music was the latest movement in the pop culture world. It was very artsy and avant guard and attracted the more bohemian, cerebral and hippy side of the student population. I found that I fit in with that group of kids magnificently. I discovered a sense of connection, camaraderie and support that I had never experienced before from a group of peers. The planning of the New Wave dance was a joyful process for me. I discovered that I really enjoyed the planning process and that I was good at it – being good at something in the school environment was a new experience.

The Friday night of the dance arrived and my friends and I were in the gymnasium decorating it in the New Wave theme and selecting the music. By the time we were done the gym had been transformed into a funky, punk-psychedelic dance space and we were ready for the night. Our planning had included a lot of advertising for the dance and we were confident that lots of students would show up. We were not disappointed. The gym was teaming with kids that night, and the dance was a big success. The decorated space, in combination with the popularity and danceability of the New Wave music that was all over the radio at the time, contributed to the popularity of the dance floor. A large percentage of the kids at the event were dancing.

At one point at the dance, I was standing off to the side with several of my co-planners and we were talking about how successful the event was. The kids were having a really good time; we had created a very special environment. It felt so good to be a part of creating such a great experience.

Then I saw them. Standing in the corner of the gym with arms crossed, clearly not dancing, grimaces on their faces and staring at me, were the neighborhood boys. Not just the neighborhood boys, but also new high school boys that they had attracted to their pack. There was a large group of them and they were staring directly at me. I felt the euphoria from the evening drain out of my body in an instant. In a flash it was replaced with a deep sense of fear and the realization that I had not escaped elementary school.

Then they approached. As they walked toward me, in a pack that was three times the size of any pack that I had witnessed before, I felt a sickness in the pit of my stomach rise up into my throat – my Complex had been activated. What I had hoped was a thing of the past, the incapacitating ball of fears that had built up over my elementary and middle school experience, came crashing down on me. Then I heard it, "Leslie the Faggot, did you make this gay New Wave thing? This music sucks and is for fags." I stood there, speechless and motionless. My new friends and co-organizers who were standing next to me heard these words and said nothing. I wondered what my new friends were thinking, "Leslie the Faggot? Is he gay?" I felt threatened and embarrassed all at the same time, and I did not know what to do. I wondered what the pack of boys would do next. Suddenly one of my new friends, the girl who was the lead organizer of the New Wave dance, moved to place herself between me and the pack of boys. She looked right at them and said in a bold and defiant voice, "Get the fuck out of here, assholes." "Lesbian!" One of the boys said back to her. "Dickhead!" She defiantly responded in return, "Get out of my dance before I get the principal and the cops." She did not back down. I was stunned and amazed at her courage and conviction in front of these adversaries. They must have sensed her resolve as they gave us the finger and then backed away.

She became a wonderful high school friend. As a matter of fact, she became the next person that I would try to make into a "girlfriend." We tried to be sexual together with various attempts to make out and get physical, but none of it resonated – for either of us. I came away from the experience more confused than ever about sexuality, but I received a much greater gift. She was the entryway into a new group of people that were supportive, kind and accepting of me. I learned that there was a whole new world of people and experiences that was outside of my elementary school experience. I could not have received a better gift at a more critical time.

## The Art of Repression

Toward the end of my sophomore year of high school I fell in love for the very first time. At the time, of course, I had no idea what was happening to me. All I knew was that I had to stuff it down very deep inside. He was a striking man with a kind, caring personality and a strong, fit and beautiful body and a handsome face. He was not a team athlete and did not participate in the high school world of athletics. He was jovial, carefree and non-judgmental. He could have very well fit into the *A list* crowd of the most popular kids, a group that I was *not* a part of, but he chose not to associate with them. He chose to hang out with the more artsy, cerebral and more marginalized segment of the class population – the group where I had found a home. Best of all, he liked me. Not in a sexual way, it was clear that he was very much into girls and had a very active sex life with his girlfriend, but in a *let's hang out and be buddies* kind of way. I adored it. We took similar classes, studied together and hung out at school. We went bike riding and listened to music and gathered with other friends on the weekends.

One day he asked me if I wanted to go lift weights together. Lift weights? I had never done this but I had always associated the activity with team sports. The old familiar shot of dread and anxiety welled up into and through my body as I contemplated the activity. I talked myself down from the emotional cliff as I realized that weight lifting was not a team sport and that I could participate with just him. I agreed and we went to the weight room. He showed me how to lift and we went through a series of exercises. I could not help but watch his body as it responded to the stress of the weights. His muscles bulged; biceps, triceps and chest all expanding from the workout. As I watched him, a fire lit within me. I felt a sensation in my groin that I had not experienced before. I was turned on – in a very big way. I walked the tightrope of staring just enough at him to satisfy the intense hunger that was burning inside me, but not too long as to tip him off as to what I was experiencing. He stood up from a set of bicep curls, pulled the sleeve up on his arm to expose his flesh and flexed his bicep in my face. "Look at how huge it is getting," he exclaimed with pride. His peaked bicep was eighteen inches from my nose. I was transported to a place of ecstasy. I had never felt the powerful kind of longing, desire, energy and attraction that overcame me in that moment. My mind went blank as I felt the intense wave of emotion come over me. I wanted so badly to touch that flexed bicep and my arm began to rise toward it. The motion activated my fears, and I froze. With the potency of a hundred crosses burning on my front lawn, the fear of being a gay person descended on me. "Leslie the Faggot," I thought. In an instant, the intense feelings of desire that I had toward my friend vanished. They were pushed down by the heavy weight of my fear; down to a place where they could not be experienced and could not be felt. Down to a place where I would not have to deal with them, or so I thought. My groin relaxed and the moment passed.

Our friendship flourished. I successfully walked the tightrope between arising sexual desire and repression of such feelings. The repression contributed to the deepening of my mental and emotional Complex; insecurity, low self-esteem, loneliness, feeling like I was not good enough and unfathomable fears and questions regarding my sexuality were enhanced. It reached a tipping point.

On one particular Saturday my parents went away for the night, leaving me with the house to myself. I invited him over and we spent the evening watching movies. We also dove into my parent's liquor cabinet, taking just a sip off of each bottle so as to disguise the intrusion. There were a lot of bottles! By the end of the evening we were buzzed, but not drunk, from the alcohol and my friend decided to spend the night. I lay down on my bed and he did too! I remember the warm feeling of him lying next to me. He fell asleep; I could not due to the electricity that was coursing through my body. And then, he rolled over in his sleep and his arm came crashing down on my chest. The same arm, the same bicep that I had so wanted to touch in the weight room had now made contact with my body. He was snoring lightly and his condition of sleep opened the door for me to *feel*, without fear of the discovery of my sexuality. My engorged penis throbbed. I allowed myself to take in the all the feelings of new discovery; raw sexual feelings – to my core. And then, just as suddenly as it had happened before, he rolled over in his sleep removing his arm from my chest. The realization and shock of what I was feeling hit me like a sledge hammer. I lay there, horrified. All of my defense mechanisms then kicked in. In particular, the notion that I was just too young and I would grow out of this *phase*. I just had not met the right girl yet and when I did all of the feelings and sensations that I just experienced with him would come to me – and then some. Like a complicated stage play, the truth of what I was feeling for him, juxtaposed with denial and repression of those feelings, acted out in my body and mind until the wee hours of the morning.

All of this came at the expense of my relationship with my best friend. My *best* friend – the boy that had been my one anchor of sanity during grade school – I had relegated to a distant friendship during this time. I was so overcome by the feelings of sexual desire for the boy that I had fallen in love with that I wanted to spend all my time with him. That left no time for my best friend. I can remember feeling bad about it but the internal drive for an intimate relationship with the boy, as repressed as it was, overcame any feelings of guilt that I had over ignoring my best friend. It even caused tension between us, which I abhorred, but it was not enough of an impetus for me to change. It could not compete with what I was feeling for the boy. I was so lost in my emotional, mental and sexual fixation that I was able to readily discard the one truly positive and enduring friendship that I had.

## Lettuce Head

Sophomore year also brought my first experience with work. My father insisted that I get a job the minute that I turned sixteen. Going to work was a highly traumatic prospect for me. I had low self esteem and even lower confidence and the thought of entering a new environment, where other neighborhood kids and peers would be present, terrified me. I saw it as just another avenue for my suffering at the hands of my peers. I was still not in a place where I would deny my father however, so I sought a job as a bag boy at the local small town supermarket, which was just a twenty minute walk from my house. I got the job and walked in the door on my first day, filled with anxiety. I was brought to the bagging area by the supervisor and there they were – two boys that had been participants in my bullying since the fourth grade. The taunting began immediately, as the boys spread the word about me. Two boys in particular, both a grade ahead of me in school, jumped on the bullying bandwagon. One of the boys gave me a new work place nickname – Lettuce Head – and it stuck. The kids loved it and Lettuce Head became the latest element in a long line of humiliations for me. To complicate things even more, I found this young man to be very physically attractive. I developed a unique and toxic relationship with him. One of fear and avoidance due to the teasing that he would instigate toward me, combined with intense sexual attraction, longing and desire for him – stuffed down deep inside so that it would not show. Another convoluted layer of dysfunction was being added to my Complex as I interacted with him in the workplace.

My work at the grocery store exposed me to lots of people. Customers in all shapes and sizes would come into the store, and I would bag their groceries and carry them out to their cars. Many of these customers were men and there were several that I found to be sexually attractive. One particular guy gave my sexual repression techniques a real run for their money. He was tall, strikingly handsome, had a very sexy mustache and, in the warmer months, would wear a tank top that would expose much of his gym sculpted upper body. When he entered the store I was transfixed and my familiar tightrope walk began. I can remember consciously positioning myself to be sure that I was the one to bag his groceries, thus maximizing the time that I would spend in his presence. All the while doing this in a stealthy and unassuming way that would not tip anyone off to my intention and desires. As he stood at the checkout counter my body would ache from the debilitating cocktail that I seemed to be drinking; a concoction of intense sexual desire mixed with powerful repression. The repression always won out, but just barely. He would walk away leaving me in a mental and emotional stupor that I would be jolted out of only when I heard the words, "Lettuce Head, you need to bag over here."

In a vain attempt to counteract all these homosexual feelings, I continued down the road of dating women and attempting sexual interactions with them. Throughout junior and senior year of high school I took women to school dances and proms and went out on dates. I even made numerous sexual attempts; make out sessions, taking off her shirt and bra and playing with her breasts. I had never gone so far as to attempt intercourse however.

Whenever I was with a girl, there was just no erection. It just never happened for me. It was senior year in high school, and I was still a virgin. I had never even ejaculated! Never masturbated! I did not even understand what ejaculation and orgasm was, really. I would date girls, unknowingly lead them on because they had sexual feelings toward me, and then I would dump them when things got too involved. I would dump them when I realized that they got to the point where they wanted a more sexual experience. I had no desire for sex with a girl, and when the deep wounds of insecurity, low self-esteem, loneliness, feeling like I was not good enough and incomprehensible fears and questions regarding my sexuality – the Complex – got triggered, *I ran*. This became a pattern, not only with girls but in life in general. Whenever difficulty in life arose, all of the elements of the Complex would come crashing down on me, and I would run from whatever was going on. Run to escape.

## Convoluted

But still I continued to try with girls. It was my senior year, and I put forth my strongest attempt yet to have sex with a girl. She had been the girlfriend of the boy that I had fallen in love with. I had become friends with her while they were dating. I can remember the boy describing to me how bountiful and pleasurable their sex life was while they were together. They had recently broken up, and I decided to move in on her in an attempt to create the same kind of sexual relationship. How fucked up was that? I had decided to date the ex-girlfriend of the boy that I was in love with! I hid this from him initially in order to not hurt his feelings. I did not want to lose his friendship and the sexual feelings it gave me.

Any straight boy would have found her very attractive. She was tall, thin and had large, voluptuous breasts. She had beautiful olive skin and long, silky black hair reflecting her Italian heritage. She was sensual. She had a way of moving that was graceful and beautiful. I found that I could appreciate all of this. We would take off in the car to the local make out view point and kiss. I was terrible at kissing. She *taught* me how to kiss as it just did not come naturally to me. We would sit in the car, with the view of the city spread out before us, and I would try. I would try so hard, but it always seemed like such an effort. I remember the thoughts in my head rapidly alternating between wondering why I did not find this pleasurable or exciting in any way, and convincing myself that I *was* enjoying it. Telling myself that I felt this sexual feeling or that sensual sensation and that it felt good. Convincing myself that this would grow into all out sexual bliss, I just needed more time, more maturity and to get better at kissing.

Then I would feel her breasts. I would feel them because I felt that that was the next logical step in the dance of sexual interaction with a girl. I would go under her shirt and try to remove the bra. I was hopelessly incompetent at removing a bra. It was such an awkward feeling and was a big source of insecurity, but, because I knew that this was the next step toward igniting my sexual feeling for a girl, I proceeded until I was successful. I would put my hands on her bare bosom. I caressed them in a way that I thought was appropriate. "Surely this would cause a reaction in me," I thought. But nothing happened. Nothing outside of the mental dance of *thinking* I was turned on juxtaposed with the fact that I was feeling nothing and that the endeavor felt like a chore. The encounter would end, as it always did with a girl, with my thoughts swirling over what was wrong with me. Why was this so uncomfortable and why did I not feel the same way that I felt about her ex- boyfriend? – the boy I was in love with!

But I kept trying. We found ourselves alone in her house one Saturday evening. We were in her bedroom, and she asked if I wanted to get into bed. This was the first time in my life that I knew that I was being presented with an opportunity to have intercourse with a girl. The thoughts in my head congealed into a swirling ball composed of curiosity and recognition of opportunity. A chance to finally have the stimulus that would bring me to that place of sexual bliss with a girl that I had heard about from my peers, the media, society and the *world*. That, combined with the insecurity and self doubt streaming from the fact that I had yet to experience any kind of sexual stimulus from being with a girl. What would happen if I felt nothing and nothing happened? Would I get an erection? What if I didn't? What if I did, and we had intercourse – would I find bliss?

Curiosity and recognition of opportunity won and I jumped into bed with her. Something inside of me really wanted this to happen. If it happened, I could feel *normal*. For once in my life I could feel a part of and the support of the entire heterosexual world. I would be able to relate, to understand, to participate in the world of hetero sex. I could have sexual conversation with others. I would understand what my male peers felt when they were looking at the Playboy magazine in their locker, or when their heads turned abruptly to gaze at an attractive girl who was walking down the street. I would finally understand the longing that I observed in the eyes of my male peers when they were holding a girl and staring into her eyes at a school dance.

I attempted with gusto. I had my chance and I decided to *grab* it. There in the bed, I caressed her as longingly and as lovingly as I knew how. I kissed her and fondled her breasts. I laid on top of her and stroked her naked body with mine. I could feel the warmth of our bodies touching and the warmth felt good. I was there, actively participating and being as present as I could. I remember feeling good about the fact that I had been able to put myself in this place and give myself this opportunity.

Nothing happened. No turn on. No excitement, no erection – no bliss. I kept trying, thinking that I just needed more time. She seemed to be enjoying herself so I remain engaged. I felt her caress my genitals and stroke my body. I felt the softness of her lips on mine. We continued along for some time and then suddenly, she reached for my penis. She felt it, and in an instant, her countenance completely changed. Her body language descended into stiffness and her caresses came to an abrupt end. She had felt that I had no erection.

In an instant, my mind and emotions went to a place of devastation. I had not been able to do it – no erection had occurred. I had experienced a prime opportunity and I had not been able to perform. My Complex erupted inside of me. The web of dysfunctional thought was interrupted by her saying, "Don't worry about it, you must just be nervous." She was being kind. I knew that she had recently experienced a wild, active and deeply satisfying sex life with her ex-boyfriend, the boy that I was in love with. I imagined that her experience with me must have been supremely disappointing in comparison. "Yea, better next time," I said. Despite the trauma, there was also tremendous relief for me because it was over. I no longer had to try to perform. However, the truth of it was, it was far from over. A deep seeded element of performance anxiety, that had already formed earlier in my life, had just been enhanced significantly. It would continue to be enhanced in a similar manner as I attempted sexual encounters with girls over many years still yet to come. This performance anxiety would manifest itself in many ways, not just sexual, as life unfurled.

She broke up with me and went back to him. In a very strange and convoluted *eighteen year-old senior in high school fashion*, we all stayed friends for the remainder of the school year. We would hang out together. The depth and the complexity of the thoughts and emotions that I experienced while I was with the two of them cannot be overstated. When we were together I would look at her and experience my insecurity, self doubt and performance anxiety. When I looked at him I would experience my sexual arousal, fear of discovery and the power of burying my feelings deep inside. All of this combined inside of me and was added to the toxic soup, the Complex, which had been concocted during the eighteen years that I had been on the planet.

## I Know Where It Comes From

I understand school shootings. I understand the violence that is caused by young people in our society. I understand how a youth can get into a place where they are completely overtaken by their thoughts and emotions and can act out from a place of unconsciousness. I understand because of the many experiences that I had from the fourth grade through high school that made me lose myself. Lose myself in the instant of a particular traumatic event, or lose myself at random due to the cumulative effects of repeated trauma being triggered somehow. On many occasions, I was completely overwhelmed by thought and emotion; completely overwhelmed by my activated Complex. During those times I know one thing for sure – I was not me. Rather, I was a physical body that had been overtaken by a toxic entity that consisted of thought patterns created by my mind and the ensuing emotional responses that those thoughts created. This created entity was dense, all encompassing and inescapable. I acted from it – from a place of unconsciousness, and not from the being that is my true self. I could not see what was happening to me when the entity became active – it just happened. It was such a powerful force that I had no choice about the actions that I would bring forth as a result of the entity exerting itself. This is why I can understand how a kid could do something as violent as walking into a school and shooting people dead. *I could have done that.* There were times when I was so lost, hopeless, desperate, angry and fearful that I could have done something far worse than my most violent act – punching an eighth grade kid in the face multiple times. I am lucky, because I did not get more violent. Perhaps this was a place where fear of my father was a gift. The fear of his wrath may have prevented me from going further. Perhaps it was just my basic nature as a non-aggressive kid. Whatever it was, I did not manifest my trauma as more violence, I internalized it instead. This entity, this Complex, I took with me as I embarked on my next journey in life.

# No Moonlight in Vermont

## The First Challenge

I had decided that I wanted to go to college. When I expressed my interest and desire to my parents, my dad said that he wanted me to go to the University of New Hampshire (UNH). As far as I was concerned, UNH was just an extension of my high school – just an additional forty-five minutes down the road. Many of my grade school and high school peers were going to UNH. I would see the same people and worst of all, they would carry my history along with them – a history that would be shared with a whole new group. I could not stomach it. I wanted, more than anything, to escape my hometown/grade school/high school world. Going to UNH would keep me firmly entrenched in that world and the thought of this was so repulsive, so fearful that it gave me the courage I needed to go against my father's wishes.

I fantasized about going to school at the University of Vermont (UVM). A new town, a new environment, three hours away by car and a whole different state. But, most of all, I fantasized about the skiing. UVM was located in northern Vermont and was near the big, famous ski resorts of Stowe, Sugarbush and Smuggler's Notch. Throughout high school skiing had become an even greater escape for me; a source of pride, accomplishment and adventure – one of the few areas of joy in my life. I fantasized about a school where I could indulge and perpetuate my passion, and UVM fit the bill.

The roadblock in this plan was, of course, my father. My father was not a supporter of higher education; he was quite vocal in his disdain for teachers, professors and the academic way of life. By sending me to UNH, he would only have to pay in-state tuition, which made him happy. If he did have to support an institution of higher learning, at least it would be the local, home grown state university. This is what I was up against and I knew it. Maybe it was age and maturity; maybe it was the need for escape, or a combination of the two that gave me the courage to propose UVM to my father. I cannot overstate how difficult it would be for me tell him that I did not want to go to UNH and that my desire was to go to UVM. I had to have a good game plan – a powerful presentation.

I had learned that UVM had a medical school and UNH did not. Ah – hah! Medicine had appealed to me and I had taken pre-med courses in high school. I could become a doctor. That would be the denouement of my UVM sales presentation to my parents. This plan would appeal to my mother for sure, as she had always held doctors in high regard. It would appeal to my father's love of money as doctors made a lot of it. I would tell them that I would enroll in the pre-med curriculum at

UVM and be on my way to becoming a doctor. It was the perfect plan.

I told them. My father told me that he would only pay for tuition that was equivalent to UNH tuition. I would have to take out student loans to make up for the higher UVM tuition. He bought it! I could tell that he did not like it, but I was going to UVM. I had stood up to my father and won. It was the first turning point in our relationship.

## A Taste of Peace Eroded by my Complex

That September my parents took me to UVM and settled me into my dorm room. My roommate had dropped out at the last minute leaving me with a room to myself. Freshness had blown into my life. I was at a place where no one knew me. No one knew my history. It was a fresh start and an intensely liberating feeling for me. With positive energy and hopefulness, I set forth to make new friends in my dorm. I was rewarded magnificently. I met several people, almost immediately, that became good friends. Hanging out in the dorm room, drinking beer and smoking pot, playing ping pong in the common area, attending parties, figuring out class schedules and class locations, exploring the new world of the UVM campus – we did this all together, and I loved it. I experienced bonds of friendship in a quantity that I had never experienced before. There was no criticism, no diminishment, no looking over my shoulder for the next threat – no bullying. During that first semester, I developed a level of confidence and self worth that allowed me to explore the world in a new way.

Several of us guys were hanging out in a dorm room

one Saturday and one of my new friends said, "Hey, let's go play football." Everyone jumped with excitement at the idea. I froze. Instantaneously I was transported to a place of fear and dread – my Complex activated. My mind told me that all the work that I had done, and this new world that I had built, were now threatened. They would discover my inability to play team sports! My thoughts rolled from there. As soon as they discovered that, they would discover Mabie the Baby, CM is Gay and, worst of all, Leslie the Faggot. I had to stop this discovery from happening no matter what the cost. Reeling within my fears, I did not have the self confidence or courage to say, "Hey, I do not know how to play. Can you teach me?" Oh, to have had the courage to have done that. How different things could have been if I had been able to get outside of my head. But the power of the Complex had taken over. Instead, I employed a technique that I had developed earlier in life – I *ran*. The running came in the form of some kind of obligation that prevented me from joining the football game. I remember leaving that dorm room to go to my phantom obligation with a very heavy heart and anxiety filled body. I was running away from my fear, trapped in an unconscious mind swirl that told me that my only option was escape – *run*! It was brutal.

After this football avoidance experience, I overcompensated. I decided that the way to escape the fear of team sports, the fear of being gay – the way to escape my Complex, was to dive head first and aggressively into student activities that were not directly sports related. I joined the Winterfest team. Winterfest was the annual campus wide celebration of winter and all that UVM and Vermont had to offer during the snow season. With my love of skiing, it was a natural fit for me. During my first year on the team I took a very active role and made a good impression. I was elected the president of Winterfest the next year. I enjoyed organizing and motivating people, planning events and coordinating activities. I was good at being the president and it was a great self esteem builder for me; I relished the positive feedback.

I really loved getting my friends involved and working with them. They supported me in the Winterfest endeavors, and that support provided me with the intoxicating joy associated with camaraderie. During one of our Winterfest planning meetings one of my closest friends said, "Hey, I'm going to form a Broomball team with the guys in the dorm." Broomball was a team sport that was like ice hockey and was played during Winterfest. Brooms were used instead of hockey sticks and boots were worn on the ice instead of skates. I had always distanced myself from this game, for obvious reasons, and delegated the organizing of it to a member of my Winterfest team. With my friend's impetus to start a team, I felt a direct threat. He went back to the dorm and proposed the team to the guys, and everyone jumped at the chance. I had been warmly included in the invitation to join the team. Half my mind and body swirled with the thoughts and emotions of wanting to be with my friends and participate in this activity with them; the other half was riddled with fear and insecurity. It was torture for me. My Complex won – I never participated in broomball. I was the master of excuses – too busy organizing Winterfest, too much studying to do, too many things going on. These excuses continued on for the four years of college, as my friends organized a broomball team and participated in the team sport every year.

It did not stop with broomball. My friends were into all kinds of team sports; soccer, softball, basketball, hockey, football. Invitations for me to participate in these activities would come regularly and I would decline, giving some made up excuse. Eventually, they stopped asking me to participate and this set off all kinds of alarms in me. Were they on to me? Had they discovered my fear of team sports, had they discovered Mabie the Sissy, Mabie the Baby and Leslie the Faggot? Had the trauma of my earlier years finally caught up with me at UVM? I was horrified.

One of my best friends at school had a family farm nestled deep in the Green Mountains of Vermont. It was an idyllic place consisting of a thousand acres containing an entire mountain valley, a farmhouse, barn and outbuildings. The place was right out of a fantasy. We would go to the farm on fall and spring weekends to enjoy all it had to offer – apple picking, cider making, maple sugaring, hiking, creating and acting out plays on the barn's stage, drinking and partying. These weekends were absolutely glorious times; a gift that I will always treasure from this life. I could never escape the call for team sports though. During one weekend my friend said, "Let's play football." There were just enough of us to form two teams to be able to play the game – my participation was needed. I felt tremendous pressure, coming from within me, to play. I did not want to let my friends down, their friendships were so very important to me. I could not disappoint them. Terror raced through my body as I decided to join the game.

# No Moonlight in Vermont

I decided to *join the game*. I did not know how to play football, and I was too self conscious and insecure to let anyone know that. So, I found myself standing in the field as my friends amassed, chose teams and took positions. All I could do was imitate their actions and that is what I proceeded to do. I watched every move they made with tremendous intensity. Perhaps if I could mirror their every move, I could pull off this charade and actually participate in this game at a respectable level.

The first play came, and I watched one of my friends dart forward and tackle the person who had the football on the opposing team. That ended the play and we took formation for the next play. I thought to myself, "I can do what my friend just did. I can run forward and tackle the person that has the football – this charade might actually work!" A partial sense of relief came over my body as I felt that I had discovered a way to participate and could actually look good doing so. The play began and I instantly ran forward and tackled the person with the football. I immediately heard a friend of mine say, in an agitated voice, "Hey, you can't do that. You ran too early and that is not allowed." Everyone was staring at me. I had obviously violated some rule that I was not aware of; I had done something wrong in this game of football, and I was being admonished by my friend for doing so.

A dagger flaming with the fire of a thousand burning crosses penetrated my heart. A staggering weakness came into my legs, bile reared up in my throat and my stomach convulsed – all from the deep pain of my fully activated Complex. It felt like their stare lasted for an eternity. I had been found out. I had been discovered – rejected. Leslie the Faggot was on full display for all to see in the middle of the field. The reality was, that my friend's comment and the ensuing stare did not last very long, and soon we regrouped into formation for the next play. I do not know how I continued to play, but I did. I noticed, with every fiber of my being, that the football never came my way and that I was always on the outside of the direct action. The game ended – it was the last time that I would ever participate in any kind of team sport at the farm.

## My Voice

I can remember diving into even more non-team sporting extracurricular activities as an escape. I became a Residential Advisor (RA) for my dorm, I joined the outing club and I joined student government. I overcompensated in so many areas except for one – studying. The pre-med courses did not resonate with me, and my studies suffered. During my sophomore year, I concluded that becoming a doctor was not for me. I did not possess the interest, drive, determination or motivation that I needed to study enough to do well in pre-med classes; C's were not going to get me into medical school.

I realized that I needed to pick another major, and the choice was clear and obvious. UVM contained a School of Natural Resources and within that school was my calling – the Recreation Management Program and its emphasis on Ski Resort Management. I remember sitting in the office of the Advisor for the Program and growing increasingly excited as I spoke to him about the curriculum. I had found my home, and I had not one single doubt about it — this is where I belonged.

There was just one very large and looming problem — my father. My, oh my — what my father would think and say when I told him that I was changing my major. After all, my argument for attending UVM revolved around the Medical School and becoming a doctor. Breaking this news to my father was a major source of stress and anxiety for me as I moved forward with changing my major. It did not, however, stop me from changing my major, which I did without consulting him. Things had changed with my father. My experiences at UVM had emboldened me with regard to my relationship with him. I had begun to stand up to him more, to question him more and to actually argue with him. Looking back, I had developed a great deal of anger toward my father, and that anger was beginning to surface as aggression toward him. I decided that I would break the news to him the next time that my parents visited me at UVM.

The visit came and during a dinner out, I told him about the new major and explained to him how excited I was about it. He was not happy. I then told him that I would need to attend UVM for an additional semester, above and beyond the standard four years, in order to complete the new curriculum. Now he was pissed. He asked me where the money would come from for the additional semester, implying that he certainly was not going to pay for it. I was ready for him on this point. I told him that the money that I was saving him on room and board by being an RA would contribute to the extra tuition needed for the semester and that I would take out student loans to make up the difference. This diffused his money argument. Then I became aggressive toward him in the restaurant. Anger rose up inside of me and poured forth. I raised my voice and told him in a very forceful and definitive manner that this change was what I was going to do. He raised his voice in return. His facial expression became stern and his body language threatening and he began to fire questions at me such as, "What the hell are you going to do with that degree?" "How the hell are you going to make any money doing that?" I responded with controlled rage. It became a real scene in the restaurant. I answered his questions with a degree of hostility, anger, drive and determination that he had never witnessed from me before. I think it surprised him. My mother became alarmed and told us to calm down and lower our voices. I stood up at the table and told my father that I was done with this discussion, my decision was made and that I was done with him. I asked him to drive me back to my dorm and to do it now. My mother was horrified. She was very uncomfortable with confrontation, anger and arguing and her discomfort caused her to spring into action. She verbally assaulted my father and told him, in the sternest manner that she could muster, that he needed to calm down and get a grip on himself. She said that she wanted to see me and spend time with her son and that she would not allow him to ruin that.

My father found himself in new territory. He had just been verbally and emotionally assaulted by his son and his wife. He had lost the argument. He had been put in his place. He asked me to sit back down at the table, and I replied in a very *loud* voice, "Are you going to be a decent human being or are you going to continue to be a shithead? If it's the shithead, take me to my dorm now!" My mother looked at my father and said to him, "I want to have a nice dinner with my son, calm down *now*." It was at that point that I learned just how much power my mother had. My father looked at her, saw the determined expression on her face and backed down. During the remainder of the dinner, my mother and I carried on with much more pleasant conversation. My dad tried to participate as best he could.

I realized something about myself after this encounter with my father. I learned how powerful my speaking voice had become. My time and experiences at UVM had caused my voice to develop as an effective tool that was at my disposal – whenever I needed it. I had become more eloquent, forceful, and convincing. I had developed a powerful verbal acuity. This was the opposite experience from my childhood, where my voice had been stifled by the events of elementary and middle school. Looking back, I realize that my speaking voice had developed in this way for a number of reasons, but probably the most powerful force behind its genesis was as a defense mechanism against my Complex. I learned that I could use my voice to partially work around the effects of my Complex, whenever life events triggered it. When fear, insecurity or feelings of not being good enough would arise, I would employ the verbal acuity that I had developed to disguise those emotions; to hide them and reduce their immediate impact. My voice became a source of pride and confidence. It served me well – for a while.

## Who Came Out?

He appeared in the class during senior year. He was stunningly handsome; he had a smile that would envelop the room with its magnetism. He had a powerful, fit and athletic body that moved with a unique combination of strength and gentleness. Being new to the class, he did not know anyone. I was instantly attracted to him and decided to *help* him by becoming his friend and easing his entry into this new world that he found himself in. For me, the attraction ended at being his friend. I had become so good at stuffing my homosexual feelings and denying my sexuality that I was able to put a cork on the allure at the friendship level. I had become a master at this corking. My actions at UVM had perpetuated the elaborate charade of my heterosexuality. I was actively dating women which kept me fully engaged in my self-denial.

We became friends. We shared a common interest in outdoor adventure activities. We hiked, skied, climbed and sailed together. We studied and partied together and became fully engrossed in the activities of the UVM campus. At the time, I was a Residential Assistant in one of the UVM residence halls. My dorm room was at the center of the floor over which I had jurisdiction – the perfect place to keep an eye on and be visible to all the students that were living on the floor.

One evening I was studying in my dorm room and there was a knock on my door. I opened it to find my new friend standing there. I was not surprised to see him as we had become the kind of friends where an unannounced drop-by would not have seemed unusual. I did however, notice something different about his manner as I greeted him and invited him into my room. As we stepped inside, I noticed that he closed the door – which was unusual and piqued my interest. There was a whiff of nervousness about him that I had not witnessed from him before – clearly something was up. He asked if we could talk, and so I took a position on the couch in my room. He sat down next to me. He was quiet and clearly struggling with something. I noticed a twitching in his lower lip as he turned his face toward the floor and hung his head; he had a tense expression on his face. His body language told me that something difficult was going on for him, and I responded by asking, "What is wrong, are you okay?" He remained silent for a moment and then lifted his head and looked at me. With a labored voice he said to me, "I am gay." The words struck hard initially. This was the first time that I had had a direct experience with a peer that involved homosexuality. The first time that I would have a conversation about being gay that was not derogatory, prejudicial or slanderous. It would be a conversation about acceptance and support, caring and understanding. The initial shock of his words began to sink deep within me, reaching for a place of unimaginable fear. I stopped the progression instantly, however. I may have hesitated after his pronouncement of his sexuality, but the hesitation was very short lived. I instantly employed all the powerful mental and emotional tools that I had developed to keep my own sexuality in check. Using my voice and body language, I responded with as much caring and support as I could, "Thank you for telling me. It is okay. I have no problem with gay people and it does not change my friendship with you." There was silence between us as I watched the words that I had spoken settle into him. He bowed his head and cried. I remember looking at the tears that were coming from his eyes and then being transported to another world. A world of intense empathy. A place of supremely deep feeling for what he was experiencing. I *knew* what he was feeling. I was looking at a mirror. The mesh of mind thought and emotion that spun up for me was about to overtake me when he looked up once again. He turned his tear soaked face to me and said, "I think I am in love with you."

It was too much. I lost myself. I became completely unconscious, unaware of the room or my place in it, unsure of what I had just heard and unable to process the depth of pain that was emanating from the face that was staring at me. And then something truly amazing happened. Empathy welled up and overtook anything else that was going on inside me. It poured forth from me as if a volcano had been stimulated into eruption. Empathy for the suffering soul that was staring me in the face. The accumulated uncertainty, questioning and fears regarding his sexuality were being overcome in the moments that were unfolding in front of me. He was taking the supreme risk of exposing himself. The empathy that I was experiencing allowed me to put all else aside and respond to him by saying, "I am flattered that you feel that way about me. Thank you for sharing it with me. I am not that way, however. I support you as my friend and I will be here for you in friendship. You do not have to worry about this conversation going any further than this room."

We sat there for quite some time – recovering. He was recovering from the effects of the supreme act of courage that he had just concluded. I was recovering from the intense internal and external play of denial and empathy that I had just acted out. We eventually lightened the air in the room with some casual conversation and music. He decided to leave, and upon his departure I said, "Thank you again for sharing with me. I do not judge you and I remain your friend. I will keep our conversation in the strictest of confidence." He thanked me and reached out and grabbed me with a hug. It lingered. He released his embrace, opened the door, turned and flashed me that million watt smile and departed. I closed the door, propped myself up against it and closed my eyes. I embarked on a stream of thought that was initially dominated by the joy of having helped someone – having *really* helped someone. It resonated in every corner of my being. The stream also contained waves of questions, uncertainty, fear and denial and they quickly replaced the joy. The mind stream of thought became a river, then a raging river. I was caught in the rapids and I was drowning in my thoughts. My Complex was activated and brought the rapids to a crescendo. Denial was my life preserver. It sprung forth attached to a long rope that dragged me to shore. My well honed tools of denial sprung into action and saved me. It all became buried deep inside. I was startled from unconsciousness by a knock on my door. I opened it to see and hear one of my dorm mates asking for assistance from his RA. I sprang into action, welcoming the distraction.

## Opening

We decided to participate in a school internship at a ski area with another classmate and scheduled the internship for the Christmas/New Year's break. We rented a large room on the top floor of an old New England farmhouse that had been converted into a B&B. It was close to the ski area and was located in a picturesque New England town. It was an idyllic setting for spending three weeks in the mountains and learning about the ski business. The three of us worked, skied, partied, and celebrated Christmas and New Year's Eve – we had a fantastic time.

On one evening, the boyfriend of the third roommate visited and the two of them decided to get a hotel room to have some private time. This left my friend and I alone for the evening. My head was spinning. During the time since his coming out to me, my thoughts and emotions had danced along the thin border between sexual repression and recognition of sexual opportunity. To date, sexual repression had remained in control, but the dance between the two had been omnipresent.

We went out into the town that evening and grabbed dinner and a beer. The air between us was heavy, our thoughts unspoken. My thoughts turned to calming my mind by getting drunk, but I could hardly stomach the one beer that I consumed, and I remained painfully sober. The evening ended by our returning to our empty room in the B&B and going to bed in our separate twin beds. As we lay there in the dark, we began to talk. He broached the topic of his sexuality. As he spoke it occurred to me – perhaps he knew, or somehow sensed, the conflict within me. Perhaps he knew that I was gay and had not yet been able to admit it or let it in. Cloaks of anxiety fell over my body as I stared at the ceiling, listening to him speak. The anxiety was not produced by fear or dread, as had so often been the case, but by the realization that I was longing for him. By the realization that the border between repression and opportunity was closer than ever to being breached. That years, *years*, of repression due to denial and fear was being challenged like never before.

He stopped talking. Like the exploding spray of an enormous wave as it crashes against a headland, the words thrust forth from my mouth, "Would you like to come over here?" I said. During the ensuing space of silent time, as tiny as it was, I felt the sensation of my body lifting off the bed. Some sort of release was occurring that I did not understand and could not fathom. His only word was, "Sure."

I turned my head to see the covers fly off his body. Dressed in only his underwear and bathed in the dim light coming in from the window, I watched his stunningly beautiful form rise from his bed and start walking toward me. He was magnificent; his muscular legs, tight abdomen, thick chest and handsome face were coming – for me. He stood over me and gently removed the covers from my body. I remembering him glancing at my form that was clothed only in underwear, and quickly descending toward me. He splayed his body out on top of mine. The total body contact that I felt sent a shock of pleasure to my core. Then he kissed me on the lips. He touched me, felt me, and gently kneaded me with his big, powerful hands. He massaged my crotch with his own. His body gently gyrated on top of me. I felt a warmth come over me that marked the beginning of a new journey in my life; an astounding journey of sexual discovery, intimacy and pleasure.

I was rocked to my core. And then I felt it, like I had never felt it before – my penis was rock hard and throbbing. It was hot, pulsing and filled with energy. My crotch was set afire as his physical presence sunk into me. My chest heaved with an explosion of energy waves that were emanating from my genitals. I gasped, I moaned, I roiled with pleasure. He knew he had me. He sensed the joy and pleasure that was radiating from me, and it turned him on. I knew that it was cathartic for him as well. "I think I am in love with you," I remembered him saying to me back in the dorm room.

We pulsed, writhed, embraced, jerked and flowed in that bed. Then we heard someone coming up the stairs toward the room. Like a guillotine severing a neck, the spell was broken. Fear of discovery by our returning roommate instantly overtook us both, and he separated himself from my body. He bolted to his bed and threw on the covers. I had myself covered back up before he even got there. The footsteps passed, headed to another room.

We lay there, speechless. My body was still pulsing from the most physical, mental and emotional experience of my life. My lungs were heaving and my mind was throbbing with thought. I heard his laden breath just six feet away. Nothing was said. Yet, everything had been said. It was now undeniable – I was a gay man. There was no question, no doubt, no wondering. The experience that I had just had was complete and total confirmation that I was gay. It was an enormously cathartic release on the one hand, and on the other it was the familiar feeling of dread as I imagined what was in store for me in life.

And then they came, like a burst of thunder – my feelings for him. All the repressed affection and fondness that I had been feeling for him since his coming out to me in the dorm room came pouring forth as I lay in that bed. It rapidly evolved into an energy that I had never felt before, and it was all consuming. I wanted him with every fiber of my being. In that instant I began to fantasize about a future together, about loving him. The combined energy of the fantasy and the sexual awakening that I had just had kept me awake into the small hours of that morning. We never spoke a word for the remainder of that night. Eventually, sleep overtook.

We awoke in the morning and hurried off to work. We did not speak of it much, but clearly our relationship had dramatically changed. Our roommate returned that day and our privacy was gone. There would not be any opportunity for any additional sexual encounters throughout the remainder of our internship. Our time at the ski area came to an end, and we returned to the UVM campus for the spring semester.

## AIDS

I returned to my duties as a Residential Assistant in the dorm. I remember entering my room for the first time that semester, and as I opened the door I thought to myself, "I am a gay man. What if the men on my floor knew this? They would reject and harass me for sure – possibly even physically assault me. All of the respect and trust that I had worked so hard to earn from them would be dashed. They would think that I have AIDS. I must keep this very tightly under wrap."

AIDS! At the time (1985) the hysteria over this new disease was rampant. It was all over the news and a deep seated fear had been implanted into the populace. Worst of all, AIDS has been strongly associated with gay men. AIDS added a whole new level of fear and anxiety to any gay man that was coming out at the time. There were so many unanswered questions – How did you get it? How was it transmitted? How contagious was it? How long would it take to kill you? I was terrified at the prospect of contracting the disease, getting sick and dying. Did *he* have it? Was I exposed to AIDS by the interaction that I had with him in the bed? Was I HIV positive now? What would my parents think? What would my friends think? Was God punishing me and all gay men for the sin of homosexuality, as so many Christian churches were claiming? Contracting AIDS would be the most humiliating thing for me – the icing on the cake of a tormented life. It was terrifying.

## 21

This fear did not stop me from seeing him, however. The desire to further the relationship and to be with him sexually was so powerful that it overcame any and all fears that were associated with being gay and the threat of AIDS. He had rented an off-campus apartment that semester and it was the perfect place for us to rendezvous. I could remove myself from my dorm, my friends and my classmates – the campus – and remain undiscovered.

The next time that we had a sexual encounter was on a cold, snowy winter night. We had gotten together for dinner, played around in the new fallen snow, and then

## No Moonlight in Vermont

he asked me if I wanted to go back to his apartment. I knew that the invitation meant some kind of a sexual experience. My thoughts and emotions became cyclonic as I wrestled with all that this invite presented; ecstasy, freedom, expression, excitement and intimacy – coupled with fear, anxiety, self-doubt, angst and AIDS. I agreed and we proceeded to his place.

His apartment was warm, spacious and inviting. I fantasized about what it would be like to live there with him. We sat down at the kitchen table to have a beer, and the nervous tension in the room was palpable. We chatted for a bit, and then he took the lead; he became the aggressor. He asked me to his bed. Without a word, I nodded my agreement. We proceeded into the dimly lit bedroom, he closed the window curtains and I sat on the edge of the oversized queen bed. I took off my clothes and lay down. I watched him remove his clothing, one garment at a time, to reveal his body. There was enough light in the room so that I could really see, for the first time, the features of his physique. He was a superb male specimen with thick, well defined and toned muscles, a chiseled jaw, vibrant blue eyes, perfect skin and gorgeous sandy blonde hair. His legs were like tree trunks – massive and powerful. His penis was thick and erect. He glanced at me with his million watt smile and I was transported – overtaken by the combination of the boiling hot, throbbing erection that was thrusting from my body and the indescribable beauty of the man that stood naked before me. He climbed on top of me and meshed his body with mine. We writhed with an energy that I had never experienced before. I felt waves of heat and tingling electricity spread over my body.

He kissed my lips, and I shuddered; the impulse coursing throughout my anatomy. My body heaved under the weight of his full body touch. I raised my pelvis into the air, thrusting my genitals into the mass of his groin. Ecstasy! I now understood the passion associated with sex that I had heard so many people talk about over the years but had never experienced.

He separated his lips from mine and slid gently down my body. I could feel his rippled abs pass over my penis as he descended. He stroked my dick with his tongue and I launched with a deep pelvic thrust in response, arching my back toward the indescribable feeling. Then he took my penis into his warm, wet mouth. I convulsed from a shock of physical ecstasy that seared into my brain. He massaged the shaft of my rock hard cock with his lips and tickled its tip with his tongue. I lay there, writhing – completely succumbing to his efforts and losing myself in an intensity of physical pleasure that I had never even come close to before.

I grabbed the hard, tight muscles of his shoulders with my hands in order to brace myself. I felt the strength of his body course through my palms. He plunged his mouth deeper onto my cock. He was now stroking the full length of my penis. He was exerting tremendous effort, and his body began to sweat. It was all encompassing.

Then it happened. I felt a force well up inside of me – a force containing such power and intensity that it startled me, even in my totally consumed state. My abdomen convulsed, my genitals tightened as if in a vice, my pelvis thrust skyward, my eyes widened and my lungs heaved with breath. My toes curled, my heart raced and my arms and hands lifted from the bed. I became frightened; I was totally out of control. *What* was happening to me?!

Then, a searing flow of energy exploded from my penis. I was having an orgasm. My first orgasm! My body shook with uncontrolled spasm as I felt a warm liquid burst forth from my dick and into the cavern of his mouth. The stupendous intensity, combined with the fear of not really understanding what was happening to me, melded to become almost painful.

It kept going! I continued to ejaculate and he continued to work my dick. On the one hand I can remember it being too much – that I had had enough and wishing that it would end. On the other, the pleasure was so intense that I did not want it to be over. Of course, it did come to an end. The orgasm eventually stopped and my body settled back down into the bed. He pulled his mouth off my penis, got up and went immediately to the bathroom. I heard him spit my cum out into the sink; harsh reality hit.

I realized immediately that he had spit out the cum because he was afraid of contracting AIDS. Semen had been identified as a possible carrier of the disease, and he was taking no chances. Did he think that I had AIDS? Did I have AIDS? My thoughts, emotions, feelings and body were instantaneously transported to a place of fear and uncertainty. It was a stark departure from the ecstasy that I had been experiencing just moments before. My mind continued with powerful momentum, and additional thoughts quickly formed. It was now undeniable – I just had an orgasm with a man, and it was my very *first* orgasm – I am definitely GAY. What will I tell my parents, what will I tell my friends, what will happen to my future? The thoughts in my head swirled as my body gradually came down from heights of physical pleasure. I was lost in an intoxicating cocktail of mind, thought, emotion and feeling when he walked back into the bedroom.

I was twenty-one years old when I had my very first orgasm. Looking back, I believe that the events of my childhood and the ensuing Complex that had formed within me kept me from being able to access the physical, mental and emotional states needed to reach orgasm. I understand now, just how powerful a Complex such as mine can be. It was capable of stopping the very potent adolescent drive toward sexual expression through orgasm. I would soon learn that it could be even more powerful than that.

He sat down on the bed, and, as if my disquiet and swirling thoughts and emotions were not enough to deal with, he broached the subject of AIDS. We talked about how they thought people were getting it and how to avoid it. He explained why he spit my cum into the bathroom sink. The energy, joy and ecstasy of the orgasm left my body. We got up, and I got dressed. We were quiet and I noticed a rather blank look on his face. I instantly understood that he was processing as much mental and emotional information as I was, and it was overwhelming him. We had both become numb. I said a nervous goodbye and headed out into the snow. I walked back to my dorm, back to my duties as an RA, back to my friends – back to my campus life. Nothing would be the same. Navigating the two divergent worlds of gay and straight was just beginning.

## 10,000 Pounds per Square Inch

I continued to confuse myself by having friendships with women that had sexual and intimate overtones. One woman in particular was in the picture during the second semester of senior year. We had developed a strong friendship and one night, when both of us were hopelessly drunk, I kissed her. I remember the internal strife that was going on when I did it. My old heterosexual world was dying, but it was not dead yet. Fear and confusion over being gay was still at work within me and, clearly, I was not yet ready to give up the hope that I might be straight and that the pain and suffering associated with being gay would end. It was terribly unfair to her. Worse yet, she had fallen in love with me and, as I would learn later, hopelessly in love with me. Our dance between friendship and intimacy continued that semester, as I continued to see him.

And see him I did – often. Our relationship deepened as we spent more time together and our sexual encounters became more numerous. I loved the attachment, the discovery, the intimacy that developed between us. It was all so new, so fulfilling, so joyous. I fell madly in love with him. I became consumed by the thought of building a life together. All of this I experienced in secrecy; no one knew about what was happening between him and me. Not my friends, not my family, not anyone.

The academic year ended and life took us in separate directions for the summer. He went back to his home, and I went to work at a summer resort in the White Mountains of New Hampshire. When we returned to campus in the fall, I was filled with excitement over the prospect of seeing him and continuing our relationship where we had left off. Quite frankly, I was longing for him sexually, intimately; I wanted us to continue on the path of building a life together.

I was shaken to my core by how I found him to be. He had changed dramatically over the summer. There was a distance relative to me. The passion, desire and longing that he had exhibited toward me was greatly tempered, and I wondered, painfully wondered, why. So I asked him what was going on, what had changed. He responded to me with five words that opened up a new, largely unwelcome dimension to my life. He said, "I think I am bisexual."

Bisexual, what was that? This was a new concept to me that I did not understand. When I asked him what it meant and how it pertained to us he responded that he was interested in sexual relationships with women as well as men. He wanted to sleep with women, as well as me. This new revelation and understanding confounded my already fragile sexual existence. I became determined to *win*. I was going to show him that I was the clear choice, that homosexuality was the clear choice, for him.

We continued our sexual and intimate relationship that semester, on and off, and I remember the constant unease of feeling like I was in some sort of contest. What would win, heterosexuality or homosexuality? Or, would bisexuality be the victor? It was a contest that I *had* to participate in, however. My thoughts and emotions were so wrapped up in being in love with him, in blossoming into the first real experience of my sexuality, that I was completely blind to the situation that I was creating and participating in. Completely blind to the dysfunctional reality that I was dating a person who was not fully into me and who was struggling with his own sexuality. The push and pull of the relationship during this time was excruciating in the polarity of the experience. At the one pole were the joy, passion, physical pleasure and sexual freedom and discovery of our intimate experiences together. At the other pole was the distance and disquiet that he would exhibit toward me as he struggled with the relationship.

I continued to approach him with the intention of *fixing* him. He would see, through his interactions with me, that I was the clear choice. The thought of losing him was devastating to me, and I worked very hard to try and find a way through to him – to *keep* him.

My dysfunction at the time was immeasurable. The conflicting emotions of my relationship with him were the perfect trigger for my Complex, and it poured forth. I actively pursued an intimate relationship with a new woman, which was a crazy, insincere, fear based relationship. I was still involved with the dance between gay and straight in an effort to obtain refuge from the fear of my acceptance of myself as gay. The relationship went nowhere, of course, and it ended conveniently when she ended up having sex with my roommate. It was the perfect excuse to end the relationship with her, which I did immediately, and I refocused my attention on him.

He took me out to my first gay bar. It was the sole gay bar in the UVM community of Burlington, VT. I can remember starting to walk across the street toward the entrance on a very cold winter night. The thoughts in my head turned to the fear of being discovered, and I remember scanning the environment with great intensity, making sure that no one I knew would see me entering the gay bar. The thought of discovery by anyone was so laden with fear that my body responded with *flight*, and I sprinted across the street, pushed open the door with great momentum and flew into the bar – nearly knocking down a bar patron in the process.

I immediately began an intense scan of the space – of this new world. It looked the same as other bars, with the one glaring exception of same sex people being physically and sexually affectionate with one another. I then received one of the great gifts of my newfound sexual existence. Looking around, I realized that I was not alone. There were others like me, and a lot of them. It was a profound sense of relief. There was a community out there that I could be a part of and find support in. I will always be grateful to him for introducing me to the gay and lesbian community in this way.

He asked me to dance. I loved to dance. It was one of the few places in my life where I felt free to express myself. I responded immediately with a, "Yes", and I entered a new world of experience – the gay bar dance floor. The music was upbeat and pounding, as was the energy in the room. I experienced, for the first time, what it was like to dance with someone that I was sexually attracted to. It was intoxicating; the freedom of movement and expression coupled with the sexual energy was overwhelming – in a very good way. I remember feeling like I had been transported to a place of great bliss; I could feel shots of energizing electricity pulse through my body. I had found a new home and I was reveling in it.

I caught her out of the corner of my eye as she lunged toward me. She was an obese lesbian dancing in high heels, and she had lost her balance. Her arm extended toward me to brace herself against my body, and in a flash the heel spike of her shoe came crashing down on my right foot. The force behind the strike was staggering. She fell on me in such a way that the entire weight of her obese body mass transferred to the heel spike and penetrated deep into my right metatarsal. As she tried to regain her balance, she pressed down – hard. I felt a searing shot of pain arc up through my foot and lower leg, and tears came to my eyes. She was oblivious to what happened; perhaps she was drunk. I will never know because as soon as she regained her balance she resumed dancing and disappeared into the darkness of the dance floor. I immediately hobbled to the nearest chair.

I sat there, with a driving ache permeating my foot and leg. He asked me if I was okay, and I said I needed to go outside for some air. I limped out the door of the gay bar and into the cold winter night. I sat down on the frigid curb, stunned from the pain and disbelief as to what had just happened to me. He again asked me if I was okay and the only response that I could muster was a, "Yes." Then he said, "Well, I should get going." He was clearly disturbed by what had just happened, and I could sense it. I said, "Okay," and he departed.

I sat there on the curb, alone in the cold night, with physical and mental pain coursing through my body. My first experience in a gay bar had started with ecstasy and concluded with agony. My mind, thoughts and emotions aligned, of course, with the agony. The thoughts in my head whirled, and my Complex activated. The train of thoughts went something like this: I was being punished for being gay; God was sending me a message, "See, if you are going to be gay I am going to punish you; This is what will happen if you continue down this road; You really are not good enough; You will be found out and rejected, You really are Leslie the Faggot."

Then the horror that was going on in my head jumped to an even higher level of trauma. I had the sudden realization that I was sitting on the curb of the sidewalk right outside the gay bar – someone might see me! I might be discovered! I need to *move* immediately. The spark of fear caused me to stand abruptly and as I did my body reminded me of what had just happened. The shot of pain that bolted through my foot and leg made it undeniable; there was something very wrong and I had to go to the hospital. How could I get there? It was up the hill about a mile away. I can't call any of my friends – they would find out what had happened, and Leslie the Faggot would be discovered – that was unthinkable. So, in the dark, subzero night I began to hobble up the hill toward the hospital. The pain was intense as I walked, but I found that if I kept the majority of the weight on my left leg that I could manage it. It seemed like it took forever to get there and an interesting thing happened along the way. I became grateful for the physical pain that I was experiencing. The pain was so intense that it consumed my attention. It took me out of the thoughts in my head. In an odd sort of way that I did

## No Moonlight in Vermont

not understand, the physical pain provided relief from the mental and emotional pain that I was experiencing.

The relief lasted until of course, I arrived at the doors to the emergency room and my mind reasserted itself. *What* was I going to tell the hospital staff had happened to me? My foot was crushed by the high heel shoe spike of an obese lesbian at the local gay bar? Unimaginable! I fabricated a new story that removed the lesbian and gay bar elements and passed it along to all the medical staff as they treated me. The doctor informed me that the heel spike of a woman's high heel shoe can exert up to 10,000 pounds per square inch of pressure. I came to learn that the right metatarsal bone in my foot was broken clean, and I left the emergency room in a cast. As I hobbled out the doors of the ER into the frigid night, crutches supporting my body weight, all I could think about was the prescription pain killers that I just took and the relief that they would soon provide. Narcotics and sleep would give me the relief that I so desperately needed.

My friend's mental and emotional distancing from me continued and grew stronger. He no longer made efforts to spend time together and one day he called and announced that he did not want to see me any longer. He ended our relationship and I experienced a new level of devastation. I now understood the pain that I had seen so many of my peers experience with regard to the breakup of an intimate relationship. For me, the pain went to the dark place in my Complex that told me I was not good enough. It also activated the defense mechanism that I had developed to deal with the effects of my Complex – it was time to *run*.

# Colorado

## Two Step

My years at UVM came to an end, and I moved from short-lived job to short-lived job in the ski industry in Vermont and New Hampshire. During this time I started to *come out* to very select, carefully chosen friends, as well as my half-sister. I had learned that my half-sister (seven years older and related to me through my father and not my mother) was a lesbian, and I divulged my sexuality to her. She was very supportive, but being 3,000 miles away in Seattle and dealing with her own life issues, our contact was minimal. To the few friends that I came out to, their response was generally supportive, but their shock was often accompanied by such statements as, "I am worried for you as I think you are in for such a hard life." I also came out to my childhood best friend. His life had taken him to college in Maine and I visited him there to break the news. His response to me was, "I am gay too!" The connection that appeared between us so strongly in the sixth grade now became stunningly apparent.

So when I decided to run, he was the person that I thought of most. I called him one day and asked him if he wanted to accompany me on a road trip west to the Rocky Mountains and beyond. The Rockies had always been a great source of dreams and fantasies for me. Those mountains were skiing Nirvana and I had longed throughout my childhood to live there, to experience them fully and live out my skiing passion.

He jumped at the opportunity. We loaded up my Volkswagen Scirocco and drove to my parent's house to bid them farewell. My parents were sad. I think they knew that once I headed west, there would be no returning East for me. My mother's face looked somber as we drove away. I had not come out to my parents; I simply could not do it. The fear that would arise in me when I would think about telling them was, and remains the single greatest mental, emotional and physical force that I have ever experienced. There was so much wrapped up in my response; rejection, disappointment, judgment, disgust, non-acceptance, not being good enough. Coming out to them was just too overwhelming. It was time to run and I drove away.

As we approached Denver, the summit outline of the Front Range of the Rocky Mountains came into view. My excitement and joy was palpable. I was fulfilling a childhood dream! It was late in the day, close to sunset, as we drove into this iconic western city. The West was a new world for us. Born and raised in New England, the sights, sounds, and culture of the West were foreign and a new discovery for us. We had no idea where we were going in the city, but we knew one thing – we wanted to find a gay bar. We drove into the parking lot of a downtown 7-Eleven, walked into the store and approached the clerk. I can remember being very nervous about my inquiry. What kind of questions could we ask this clerk that would give us the information that we needed to find the gay bar, without using the word gay and tipping her off to the fact that we were homosexuals? You see, at that time in the mid 1980's during the full blown AIDS crisis, it was still very dangerous to be labeled as gay. It was not possible to know what harm, if any, could come to you upon the revelation. The threat of harm was very real, and we felt a strong need to remain under cover. She was an African American woman dressed in psychedelic clothing and laden with flashy jewelry. Somehow, I felt safe with her, and I found the strength to utter these words, "Do you know of any fun, funky, kind of eclectic bars or dance clubs in the area?" She glanced at us quickly, gave us a smile and wrote down the name and address of a dance club nearby. She said it would be what we were *looking for* and she wished us a good time. She had pegged us instantly as gay men. An enormous sense of relief came over me and I thanked her profusely as we departed the store. We got into the car, looked at each other and broke out into stress-relieving laughter as we realized that she knew, without a moment's hesitation, that we were a couple of gay guys looking for a good time.

It is difficult to describe how deeply the interaction with this woman affected us. Something as simple as asking for a recommendation and directions to a bar was profoundly difficult in our young gay man world. Moving through straight society in a stealth manner, with fear of discovery as your constant companion, was a lot of difficult work. To have a complete stranger understand us immediately, provide no judgment or rejection and actually *help* us in a kind manner was a profound experience.

One should never underestimate the power of a single act of kindness. I learned the truth of that statement at the 7-Eleven. Her impact on me was fervent, and I shall always remember her as a true light in my life. The first stranger to acknowledge my sexuality and still treat me with dignity and respect.

We drove into the parking lot of the club and our senses were immediately assaulted by a plethora of new sights. There were guys hanging out in the parking lot dressed in cowboy hats, western style shirts with bolo ties, shiny cowboy boots and thick leather belts with enormous silver and turquoise belt buckles. The music emanating from the club was a funky mix of cowboy country western and disco. I remember feeling *very* out of place and self conscious as we walked through the parking lot in our tee-shirts, shorts and sneakers – our typical East Coast summer wear.

I grasped the horseshoe handle, opened the heavy wooden front door, entered the club and looked around. I felt like I had stepped onto a classic Western movie set. Everything was wood – big timbers formed the ceiling and old barn planks coated the walls and covered the floor. The space was decorated with every kind of western object imaginable – branding irons, saddles, lanterns, cowboy boots, wagon wheels, coyote and wolf taxidermy. There were men hanging out everywhere and being affectionate with one another – yup, it was definitely a gay bar – thank you 7-Eleven clerk.

And then there was the dance floor; unlike any dance floor I had ever seen. It was constructed like and appeared to be just like a western horse corral – the kind you would see at a rodeo or on a ranch. A heavy wooden fence ornamented with hitching post hardware surrounded the dancing space. We cautiously moved to the fence, folded our arms across the top rail, leaned against the hard wood and cast our gaze onto the dance floor. It was loaded with couples dancing together to the sounds of a country and western song. The dance was unusual; like nothing we had experienced before. Couples were moving clockwise in a circle around the floor, kicking their toes, stomping their feet and tipping their cowboy hats in unison. My friend went to the bar to get us a drink. I stood there, feeling like all eyes were on me and sticking out like a sore thumb dressed in my casual East Coast summer attire, when I felt a brush against my arm.

When I glanced to my right to determine the source of the touch, I saw him smiling at me. My head pivoted back left, then immediately turned back to right as my brain processed what I had just seen. He was gorgeous, and he was looking at me. He had intentionally brushed up against me to get my attention. He extended his hand to greet me and introduced himself. He was tall, powerfully built, ruggedly handsome with a chiseled face, warm eyes and a gleaming smile. He had flowing, sandy brown hair, and his skin was tanned from the sun. He wore a denim shirt and jeans, cowboy boots and a cord choker necklace. When I shook his outstretched hand I felt the power of his grip and the enormous size of his palm.

We stood there and talked for a bit, introducing ourselves. My friend returned with our drinks and the introductions continued. Then he asked me to dance! Dance?

"I don't know how to do this kind of dance," I replied. He responded, "Don't worry, I will teach you." He grabbed my hand and led me through the crowd to the edge of the dance floor. He showed me the basic foot movement for the *two step* dance. "Slow, slow, quick, quick," he would repeat as he demonstrated the stepping sequence. Then he said, "Don't be nervous and just follow my lead." He grabbed my waist and thrust us into the flow of the moving dancers on the floor. I felt the confidence of his powerful forearm and hand as he guided my body. Slow, slow, quick, quick – I found the movement to be quite easy and satisfying. More satisfying was experiencing him as we moved across the floor. He held me firmly and tightly, he smiled gently at me and gazed at me with his piercing bright blue eyes. I could feel the strength in his upper body as my hands clasped his shoulder and waist in the dance pose. He was fit and athletic and it showed in his movements. The dance with him was a truly miraculous experience. Learning a new dance (remember, I loved to dance) in a new setting in my newly discovered fantasy world of the Rocky Mountain west *and* in the arms of a beautiful gay man who was clearly interested in me, was a mesmerizing experience.

My friend had also found a dance partner and seemed to be keeping himself occupied. At least that is what I thought. It was obvious to me that he saw what was going on between me and this guy, and he was giving me the space to explore it. He kept himself occupied all night; I shall always be grateful to him for supporting me.

We danced the night away. We shared our histories over

beers while leaning against the corral. We bonded. I was transfixed, and so was he. I told him that my friend and I were headed out of town tomorrow to continue our journey west. We were headed for Rocky Mountain, Grand Teton and Yellowstone National Parks.

He told me that he was heading up into the Colorado Rockies tomorrow to secure a job for the upcoming ski season. My heart skipped a beat when he told me this. I told him that it had always been a dream of mine to spend a ski season in the Colorado Rockies. Then he uttered the words that would greatly alter the path of my life. He said to me, "Why don't you join me? We could get a place together." I felt my insides come alive with excitement at the thought of it. A winter skiing in the high Rockies, with *him* – this new, gorgeous man that I seemed to be having an instant connection with. My mind played out the fantasy for the rest of the night. There was no denying it. I was going to move to the Colorado Rockies and spend a winter skiing with this hunk.

The evening ended when my best friend and I realized that it was the wee hours of the morning and we still had a several hour drive to reach our campsite at Rocky Mountain National Park. As I said goodbye to the stunning man that I had just made such a powerful connection with, I told him that I would be back to Denver in the fall. At that point we could find a place to live and move up into the mountains. As we parted, he looked at me longingly with his piercingly beautiful blue eyes. It was a look that I would carry with me for the next several months.

## Elevation

My best friend and I continued our journey throughout the west. When September arrived, we parted ways in Salt Lake City. He was destined for California, and I was headed back to Denver. Understanding my intense longing for the man I met in Denver, he made accommodations to take a bus to California and then fly back East. It was a major concession that he made for me as the original plan was for us to drive together, in my car, all the way to California. I thanked him, but not enough. I am still grateful to him, to this very day, for what he did for me.

I drove back to Denver and we met in a parking lot in the city. He had secured a place up at a ski resort for the winter; his truck was loaded with his belongings, and he asked me to follow him on the drive up into the mountains. As I followed him up I-70, the mountains rose on all sides of me. It was one of the most exciting times of my life. I was setting myself up to live in the Colorado Rockies, at a ski resort, with a gay lover! I simply could not contain my excitement and joy as 12, 13 and 14,000 foot peaks stretched skyward all around me. The intensity of the cobalt blue Colorado sky struck me as the highway crested an 11,300 foot pass. We stopped at the pass to admire the scenery. I stepped out of the car, felt the cool crisp air on my face, spread my arms wide, tilted my face to the sun and experienced glee. I then looked at him standing in front of me, and experienced bliss. He moved toward me and hugged me; he was participating fully in my excitement and joy. His strong embrace triggered a physical response in both of us. The sexual energy that was introduced into the moment delivered us into our own world – a world that was quickly challenged by the slam of a car door near to us. Someone else had arrived to admire the view. The fear of discovery quickly overtook us, and we retreated back into our platonic relationship roles. But the sexual fire had been lit.

Our appointment to see our new home was not until the next day, and we planned to camp for the night. We arrived at the campsite – a gorgeous, private spot in an aspen grove at the foot of a gleaming, conical peak. As we set up the tent, I looked around and felt as if I was in a dream. The mountain scenery, the clean air, the sounds of the rustling aspen leaves in the wind and the sexual energy between us was intoxicating. We could hardly get the tent set up fast enough in anticipation of sex. We threw in our sleeping bags, jumped in the tent and threw off our clothes. His body was a masterpiece – fit, muscular and beautifully tanned. A thin coating of hair covered his broad chest and cascaded in a slim ribbon to his genitals. His penis was thick and engorged – he was *very* turned on. We melded and writhed in the pleasure of our full body touch. I shuddered with ecstasy as the sensations overtook me. I placed my body over him and powerfully pressed my genitals against his. He grasped my dick with his brawny hand and stroked me hard; I arched my back and thrust my head and shoulders toward the sky in response to the intense pleasure. He arched his back, lifting it off the floor of the tent, and thrust the combined weight of his body and mine skyward – an incredible display of strength. I was turned on beyond my wildest dreams. My abdomen convulsed, my balls tightened in a vice, my face winced, my body seized and my penis erupted into orgasm. I ejaculated all over his tight, muscular abs. His body acted the same in turn, and he yelled out with intense pleasure. As I rolled off of him, heady from the afterglow of an intense orgasm and sexual experience, I barely noticed something odd – he did not ejaculate. I asked him why he did not ejaculate and if there was anything more that he would like me to do. He shared with me that it was difficult for him to achieve orgasm and ejaculate. He asked me to please not take it personally; that it was no reflection on me. He was clearly bothered and embarrassed by this. I felt intense compassion for him as I identified strongly with sexual repression and the inability to *perform*. I don't remember my exact words to him, but I know that I expressed my understanding and acceptance. I think he felt my compassion and lack of judgment and he became at ease. It was a powerful bonding moment for us. I did not know for sure why this gorgeous, healthy and fit gay man had difficulty with reaching orgasm, but my strong suspicion was that it had something to do with negative self judgment and shame over being gay. We lay there in each other's arms for quite some time, reveling in each other and listening to the sounds of the forest. We eventually rose, dressed and set out to explore the gorgeous alpine meadow that was adjacent to our camp.

## Caretaking

The next day we travelled out to the house that he had found where we would live. We drove up a long gravel driveway, rounded a corner, crested the hill and there at the top of the rise it stood. It was a massive, modern home with heavy wood beam construction. Large, floor to ceiling windows gleamed in the sun. From its perch high on the hill, the house had views in all directions; to the east were the snow white peaks of the continental divide, to the south rose the ski area with its ribbons of trails coming down the mountain, the west and north expanded with open mountain vistas. The home was similar in style, design, look and grandeur as the signature lodges located in our national parks.

After my first look at the exterior of the home, I glanced at him in disbelief and said, "This is where we are living? How much is the rent?" He laughed and then explained to me the situation. The home was owned by a wealthy Denver family, and it was their second home ski house. Within the house was a caretaker's apartment, and we were going to live in that apartment and *be* the caretakers. He said that in exchange for caretaking duties, we would be able to live there for minimal rent – $280.00 per month!

I was stunned and amazed, and my excitement grew as I learned of this opportunity. He said, "Come on, let's go inside." The interior of the house was as beautiful as the exterior. A gourmet kitchen with granite countertops and Viking appliances, a great room with soaring ceilings and big comfortable couches, a dining room with gorgeous Stickley table and chairs, multiple bedrooms and bathrooms. And everywhere windows. Big, soaring windows that showcased the views in all directions.

Then he took me to the caretaker's apartment. We ascended a circular metal staircase into the roof section at the back of the house. At the top of the stairs he unlocked the door, and we entered. The apartment consisted of three rooms; the first contained the kitchen, dining area and sitting area, the second room was our bedroom and the third the bathroom. It had windows in the kitchen and bedroom giving us access to those wonderful views. It was adorable. It was perfect for the two of us. He asked me how I liked it and I could not contain my enthusiasm. I said, "I love it," and threw myself into his arms and thanked him for finding such a special place for us. He then shared with me the list of caretaker duties, which was remarkably simple and involved minimal work. All we really had to do was keep an eye on the house and clean it and do laundry after a family visit. The family told us that they planned on using the house only two or three times that season so our caretaking task would be very easy.

"Let's move in," I said to him, and we headed down the spiral staircase destined for our cars and our belongings. At the foot of the stairs he turned to me and said, "Oh, I forgot one thing. The family told me that we can use and enjoy the whole house when they are not here." I had to pinch myself. We could use and live in this spectacular home.

Out at our cars he grabbed an armful of his stuff and headed toward the house. As I watched him walk I had a startling moment of realization. The full picture of what I was experiencing hit me. I was living in the Colorado Rockies, at a ski area, in a magnificent home, with my *gay lover*! It was childhood fantasy come true. I was experiencing it. It was *real*. I loaded my arms with my possessions, walked across the driveway, through the door of the house and into my new life.

## Can I Join You?

The aspens turned golden, and the first snows came to the high country. We had settled in nicely to our new home and to each other. We had set off to find jobs and had been successful. He lined up work as a ski instructor at the mountain, and I landed a front desk job at a resort hotel.

The late fall and winter were full of bliss for me. On our days off, we skied our local mountain, traveled to and skied other areas and went to Denver for nights of partying in the gay bars. I adored him and this wonderful world he was sharing with me.

My parents came to visit for a week during January. We arranged our apartment with two beds, creating the impression of a bachelor pad, and I continued on with being *in the closet*. There was just no way that I was capable of telling my parents that I was gay. He remained a roommate, barely noticeable in the shadows during their visit. He did not like it, but had a cautious understanding.

One winter weekend he and I travelled to another town and ski area and stayed at a gay bunkhouse. It was my first experience staying in a gay lodging establishment, and it made me nervous. I was scared of coming into contact with and contracting AIDS. I was also concerned about someone making sexual advances toward him. He was so attractive and the sexual atmosphere in the bunkhouse was so open and free that a sexual advance toward him was a real possibility. What would I do if it happened? What if a *three way* presented itself? I felt tremendous jealousy and possessiveness toward him, and I wanted him all to myself.

We went out and had a wonderful dinner, just he and I. We returned to the bunkhouse and retreated to our loft bedroom. To access the space we had to climb a ladder and emerge through a hole in the ceiling into the attic space of the house. We then crawled over to the large, circular bed that was draped in soft red linens and piled high with big down pillows. It was a sex pad – no doubt. There was no way to close up the hole that led to the room.

We were hot and horny for one another, quickly undressed and started sexually pleasuring one another. I was getting really excited when I heard the creak of wood at the ladder. I turned my gaze toward the hole in the ceiling that allowed for access to our space and saw a man staring at us. Only his head from the eyes up was visible as he peered at us. All of a sudden he asked, "Can I join you guys?" To my surprise, my partner said immediately and in an excited voice, "Sure, come on up!" I felt intense fear and rejection. Was I not good enough? Why did he need this other man? I was not strong enough to voice my objection; my insecurities took control. My mind whirled, my emotions spiked and my erection sagged. I was so hurt and could not control my despair. Our guest must have sensed the negative energy coming from me and the excited energy coming from my partner. He launched himself at my partner and thrust his penis into his mouth. I watched in horror as the stranger gave a blow job to the man I loved. And then the unthinkable happened – my partner had an orgasm. As he convulsed, the stranger took his rock hard penis out of his mouth. I heard a *slap* as his stiff dick hit his abdominal muscles. And then he came. He came long and hard and his cum ejected out of his penis and landed all over his torso. The depth of my anxiety grew as I watched the stranger reach for his own dick, stroke it and ejaculate all over my love. I sat there, with my back against the cold attic wall, my dick limp, my ego shattered, and a weak smile on my face that attempted to hide the terror.

He *came*! He had never ejaculated with *me*. My Complex filled me with thought and emotions laden with shame, inadequacy and not being good enough. What was wrong with me? Why did I not turn him on enough to orgasm and ejaculate? I was riddled with emotional pain as the visitor slowly composed himself, and said, "Thank you," to my love, glanced at me with a nervous look, slowly made his way to the ladder, climbed through the opening and disappeared into the night.

We lay there motionless and silent. The nervous energy between us was palpable. I was frozen by insecurity and fear. His face was red from the flush of orgasm and he was still breathing deeply and rapidly. Understanding what had just happened and the implications, he looked at me and said, "Don't worry. It is all right. Let's get some sleep."

He dozed off quickly. My whirling, spinning mind kept me awake long into the night, torturing me with the incessant clanging of mind stuff. Finally sleep overtook; the escape of sleep was never more welcome.

## Rocky Mountain Low

The drive back to our home the next day was filled with nervous silence. We both had been deeply impacted by what had happened the night before. I found the courage to broach the subject, and I asked him, "What was it about last night that triggered your orgasm?"

He responded, "I don't know. Maybe it was the energy of the third person, maybe it was the right time and place. Don't worry about it."

My Complex activated, and I became agitated, raised my voice and replied, "Don't worry about it?! We have been sexual many times and you have never been able to have an orgasm with me. How do you think that makes me feel?"

"I don't know; just don't worry about it," he said with a raised and agitated voice.

"Well, can we try something different next time? Something different that will excite you?"

"I don't want to talk about this anymore. Just drop it," he exclaimed.

"How can I just drop it? I am just trying to understand and make things better."

"Forget about it," was his reply.

He had reached a point where he was not going to discuss the subject any further. We were both angry, and we retreated into an uncomfortable silence for the next two hours, all the way home.

Something had changed. The month of February brought a distance to our relationship that had not been there before. I sensed it, but was too afraid to talk about it, too afraid of upsetting him and losing him. I remained silent about the change in his affection toward me. Sex became infrequent. He travelled to Denver on several occasions, telling me that he was setting up work for the upcoming summer. I was not invited to make the trips with him.

He returned one evening from one of the Denver trips, walked in the door and said, "Hello, we need to talk." Then these words came from his lips, "I don't want to see you anymore." He continued, "I want to live here for the remainder of the ski season, and then I am moving on. We need to sleep in separate beds now." He said it just like that. As matter of fact and emotionless as could be. As I sat there, taking in his words, I felt the dark cloud of despair settle in on me.

I asked him, "But why? What is wrong? What did *I* do wrong?"

He replied, "I have fallen out of love with you and now I need to move on – that's all."

"Is there something I can do to make it better between us? Are you willing to try? I am willing to try!"

"No," he replied. "I am done with this now and I am moving on. You need to move on too."

There was a firmness and conviction in his voice that told me that any further attempts on my part would be useless. It was clear – he was done with me.

He said, "I need to go now. I am meeting some friends for a drink."

He walked out the door. I sat there, stunned. All I could do was feel the Complex in me activate. I felt rejection and inadequacy. I felt, with great certainty, that I was not good enough. The pain permeated my body from head to toe. I remained there, for I don't know how long, in stunned, motionless silence. Eventually I got up, walked over to *our* bed, picked up my personal belongings and moved them to the other bed – the bed that, from that night on, would be *my* bed alone.

We lived in the same space for another month, until the end of the ski season and the completion of our jobs. During that time I learned from a mutual friend that he had found someone else. He had met another guy and had left me for him. The guy was running a tourist train up in the mountains above Denver and that is where my love had been spending his free time.

It was torture for me to exist in the same living space with him. Seeing him come and go, knowing he was sleeping with another man, making small talk and pretending like I was okay – all of this drove my despair ever deeper. During that month though, I can remember myself silently thinking and hoping that if I could just be cool, kindly, funny and attractive that he would change his mind. It might not be over. He would see the error that he was making. Every ounce of physical evidence during that month pointed to the fact that he was done with me and our intimate relationship. I was blind to it. My insecurities were so deep that my mind was capable of weaving stories that would completely deny the facts. Completely deny the truth, the present moment and what actually *was* by weaving a tapestry of thought that was capable of convincing me otherwise. I held out hope.

His job actually ended early. The ski season had a quick end due to unusually warm spring weather, and he had been released from the ski school for the season. When I came home from work that afternoon, I found him packing up his belongings. He was almost done when I arrived. From the window of our bedroom I watched him complete the task of loading his truck. He shut the door and then walked toward the house. I heard his footsteps on the metal spiral staircase as he ascended toward the apartment – our apartment.

He walked in and looked at me. I stood there, frozen with anticipation. Was this goodbye; the end; done? Or, was this, "See ya later; I just need a break for a while; here is where I am going and this is my phone number – I will see you soon; come visit me, please?"

He said, "Well, this is goodbye. I am moving to Denver. I hope you have a good rest of the season."

I found myself incapable of speaking. He walked toward me and gave me a hug. A quick, insincere hug goodbye – our bodies barely touching. He then turned, walked out the door and disappeared down the spiral staircase.

There was no "Here's my number." No "Here's my address." No "See ya soon." No "Let's keep in touch." It was a clean, complete and total break – as severe in its nature as it could possibly be.

I walked to the window and watched him get in the truck. The sun had set and darkness was falling. He started the truck, turned on the lights, drove down the gravel driveway in a cloud of dust and disappeared from my life.

## The Discovery of Space

I stood at the window, motionless and numb. It was done. The fantasy – Colorado Rockies, ski resort, gay lover, was done – over. It had not worked out. My mind whirled at the thought of it. Many thoughts came, like a freight train, and were followed by their corresponding emotions. What had I done wrong? – Insecurity. What should I have done better? – Self doubt. I am a bad person – see what God does to gays? – Humiliation, shame and fear. I am alone – rejection and loneliness.

This last one, I am alone, hit the hardest of all. You see, in all this time, I had actually come out to very few friends. The only member of my family that I had come out to was my sister, and she was far away in Seattle, and we did not have much of a bond. I felt as though I had no one to reach out to. No one to go to for support. The thought of coming out to anyone at this point in time was unthinkable. I was so completely overwhelmed by what had just happened to me that the thought of revealing my sexuality to anyone, and the resulting trauma that the process would cause, was way beyond anything that I was capable of doing. I stood there, alone on a Colorado hilltop, thousands of miles from anyone I knew or anyone that cared about me. I felt crushed, dumbfounded, devastated and worst of all, separated from the world. I felt agonizingly alone.

My body felt weak and sick; I had to sit down. I leaned my back into the chair and the descent began. My mind took me down the path of reviewing the entirety of the trauma that had occurred in my life. Leslie the Faggot, the burning cross, team sport humiliation, physical and verbal abuse, repressed sexuality, failed gay relationships, secrecy and repression. My thinking mind was a very powerful thing; it dragged me along like a wild river. I was deep in the rapids as my mind churned up the memories and the associated emotions, one by one, painful event after painful event. My Complex was activated to a depth and intensity that I had not experienced before. If I had been conscious of the Complex, which I was not, I would have been able to see that I was actually adding to it, building it and making it stronger as I sat there in the chair, my mind and emotions in full onslaught.

I began to sob, then cry, then cry hard. I simply could not deal with the level of pain and fear that I was experiencing. It was devastatingly cumulative, overwhelming and there was no relief. The totality of my existence, sitting there in that chair, was consumed by a thick, oppressive darkness. A weight so heavy and domineering that my mind, quite suddenly, turned to a single focus. Maybe it is an ingrained, instinctual response that works like the kill switch on a steam boiler when the pressure gets too great, but whatever the reason, the single focus that my mind settled on was relief. Relief from the unbearable mass that was pressing down on me. Relief at all costs. Relief by whatever means.

My dad had sent it to me as a gift, in order to keep me *safe*. It was stored out of sight under the bed. I got up from the chair and retrieved it, along with the box of ammunition that lay beside it. I sat back down in the chair, opened up the double barrel of the shotgun and loaded two shotgun shells into the black holes of the shot chambers. I turned the gun around, placed the butt of the stock on the floor in front of me and pointed the barrel at my face.

Relief. All my mind could tell me was to get *relief*. Relief was looking at me. All I had to do was pull the trigger. The insanity, pain, fear, self-doubt, humiliation, abuse, repression and secrecy would end in the blink of an eye. The unobserved mind is such an incredibly powerful force. It had brought me to the brink of destruction.

I reached down and placed my finger through the trigger hole. I closed my eyes. A simple twitch was all that was necessary and it would be done. My finger touched the gold metal trigger. It was cold.

How the *One Force* enters this world was a mystery to me at the time. At that moment, it came to me as the cold. The cold of the gold metal trigger. It startled me into a moment, a very slim moment, of not thinking. Something so fleeting, yet so powerful. This moment of not thinking resulted in a momentary lapse of emotion as well. The lack of thought and emotion somehow opened the tiniest space for something else to come in. In that empty space, I felt the presence of a deep peace. Tiny and fleeting, but there. It was a force, a single, all pervasive *One Force* and it changed the direction of my actions. My mind, startled out of its incessant thinking for just a moment, began to think again, but this time in a new direction. And that direction manifested into a single thought. The thought was, "This just has to get, and will get – *better*."

The tears were rolling down my face as I pulled my finger away from the cold gold trigger. The absence of the cold startled me into a moment of not thinking, once again, and the *One Force* reappeared in that non-mind occupied space. I would learn more about this *One Force* in the time to come. As I returned to thinking, I realized that it was time to no longer be alone. I knew that I had to start coming out to, and being more honest with, my friends; I had to find support for this journey. I felt a sliver of peace. I felt a new direction. A new mission.

I cocked open the gun's ammunition chamber and removed the two shells. I placed them back in the shell box, got up from my chair and stored the shotgun back under the bed. I grabbed a pad of paper and a pen and set about to write a coming out letter to a friend.

But to which friend? I had been blessed with many. Whom could I really trust? – There were many. Who would accept me and who would reject me? – Unknown. Who had space in their life to lend me support? – A few. I chose a college friend who, at the time, was living in Mali, West Africa and working for the Peace Corps. It was an agonizing write. I felt as if I needed to bare my soul in order to give a complete explanation of my sexuality. The challenge was that my soul was clouded by the numerous penetrating elements of my Complex, and the writing brought forth a great deal of anxiety. Despite it, I wrote. I wrote into the wee hours of the morning, working and reworking the text. I can remember watching and feeling my hands shake as I sealed the completed letter in the envelope. I got up from the chair and walked into the bedroom, my balance unsteady, and collapsed onto my bed. I was completely spent from the events of the evening and drifted off into the peace and escape of sleep.

The next morning I went to the post office and adorned the envelope with the necessary postage to get it to Mali, West Africa. I walked to the outgoing mail slot, raised the envelope to the opening, and hesitated. Would I get support or would I be rejected? Should I really send this to him? Would I lose a friend? How many friends will I lose if I follow this path of coming out? I felt intense fear as I stood there motionless, the tip of the envelope perched on the lip of the mail slot. All of a sudden, from behind me I heard a voice. "Excuse me sir, are you all right?" said the woman who was standing behind me, waiting to put her mail in the outgoing mail slot. Startled back into reality and realizing that I was holding someone up, I pushed the letter into the slot. I said, "I am fine, thank you. Sorry for the hold up," and I walked away.

# Vocal Cords

## How Fast Can a Person Run?

I walked out to my car, opened the door and sat in the driver's seat. Out the front windshield lay a view of the Colorado Rockies. I noticed that, as I looked at them, they had lost their luster. The joy and excitement that these mountains had generated for me when I first arrived in the high country had been replaced by a sensation of emptiness. I began to think about what I needed to do next with my life. I felt very alone, insecure and directionless and, unfortunately, made a decision from that very unclear place.

I decided to go back home. Back to that small town in New Hampshire. Back to the scene of the entire childhood trauma. Back to my parents. My dad had his small business designing and installing kitchens and baths, and he had hoped that, at some point, I would come back and take it over. There in the seat of the car, staring at the peaks, I decided that I would do it. It was a decision made from the ambiguity and obscurity of my Complex. A decision made on the basis of finding some safety. A decision made from being unable to remove myself from the mental formulations of my mind and the toxic emotions that resulted. A decision made based on a very poor foundation, but a decision I made nonetheless. Incorrectly once again,

I decided that running was the answer. When I called my parents and told them of my decision, they were giddy with excitement.

I finished out the last couple weeks of the season at my job, packed up my belongings, loaded my car and drove down the driveway. As the house, *our* house, fell out of sight my mind was flooded with the memories of the past year. Heading east on the interstate, I crossed the Colorado border, leaving the Rocky Mountain State behind. Tears were streaming down my face.

Of course it did not work out. Predictably, it did not last long. My father tried hard, and I give him much credit for that. But I was a mess, still completely engulfed in the dysfunction of my mind, my emotions – my Complex. It was tough trying to live as a gay man in the closet in New Hampshire in the mid 1980's. After three months I told my parents that I could not take over the business. I told them that it was not the life that I wanted. He and my mom were crushed, I know.

Again, I ran. This time to live in Boston. It lasted two years and the pattern continued. I even tried to have sex with a woman again, unsuccessfully – crazy! I ran to New York City to live with a guy. It lasted three months. Again, I ran. This time, I took the sum of my worldly possessions, which fit into two suitcases, and boarded a Greyhound bus bound for Seattle. For three days I traveled on that bus, arriving in the Emerald City to my awaiting sister. I had arranged to live with her until I could get my feet on the ground.

The madness was all encompassing, and finally I cracked. The mental and emotional turmoil was so persistent and dogged that I finally reached a point where I decided to see a mental health counselor, to try and find some relief. It did not work out as I did not gel with the therapist, but it was significant in that I had taken my very first step on a long road of positive discovery.

## Positivity – of a different sort.

In Seattle I continued on a roller coaster of dating man after man. I met one that I fell in love with. We shared a love for the natural world and we spent two years exploring the mountains of Washington State. He did not want a romantic relationship with me, and he made that clear from the start. He was not in love with me. Gradually, I became comfortable with just a friendship and stopped seeking anything more. It turned into a remarkably beautiful friendship. In addition to exploring the natural world, we became involved in preservation efforts; I admired his drive and tenacity with regard to environmental preservation.

One day we were on a hike in the Cascade Mountains. It was a sunny, glorious midsummer day and we had just arrived at the summit of a peak. We sat there, just the two of us, gazing at the labyrinth of peaks and valleys that spread out before us. We were in awe. Then he said to me, very quietly, "I have AIDS."

I looked at him. I filled with angst as the news swept over me. Here was this beautiful, intelligent, passionate man – the picture of youth, health and vitality – revealing to me that his body contained *the* disease. *The* frightful disease that had been constantly simmering in the background of the lives of all gay men, including my young life. Now here it was, front and center.

I said in a panic, "Are you sure? How do you know? Have you been tested?"

He replied, "I was tested a year ago and was positive. I have the first symptoms – lesions on my skin on my back."

"Tested, positive, lesions – my God, it is true and real," I thought to myself.

I sat there, dumbfounded. I knew that it was a death sentence. This beautiful friend, a man that I loved, had come into my life and would be here for only a very short period of time. It was an excruciatingly painful realization.

I needed and wanted to show him support. All that I could muster to say to him was, "I will be here for you. I love you, and I will do whatever I can to support you."

He sobbed, and then broke down into a waterfall of tears. His level of pain was intense and deep, I could sense it so well, perhaps because I had had my own experience with deep pain. I ached with sadness and concern for him. I put my arm around him, and we remained there on the summit for quite some time, sitting in silence.

The hike down was quiet. We got back to the car and I reiterated to him my support. I said, "Please know that I will do whatever I need to do to help." I had no idea of the ride I would be taking over the next year as the disease unfolded in him.

It was during that next year that I met the love of my life. He came in a way that was unique; in a way that I had never experienced before. He actually pursued me! I was so caught up in the world of support that I was giving to my friend with AIDS that, for the first time in my life, I did not have the drive or the energy to pursue a relationship with a man.

I rebuked his advances, but he was persistent. I knew something about this encounter was different, as he was physically gorgeous and I felt attraction, but I did not desire to do anything about it. That was a first.

His persistence and my lack of interest resulted in a long, slow process of getting to know one another – another first for me. At his insistence, we did not have any sexual interaction until many months into our dating relationship – another unique experience for me. The relationship evolved slowly and encouragingly. He understood what I was dealing with regarding my friend who was suffering from AIDS, as an ex-partner of his had AIDS as well. We would talk about our experiences with the disease, how it was affecting those we cared for and how it was affecting us as caregivers. We found great support in one another; that support would carry us through much of what was to come. He became my partner.

## Masses

I had just turned twenty-nine years old. My friend was dying of AIDS – the disease now in full manifestation, and I was providing support. My Complex was well developed, active and producing all sorts of negative ramifications in my life. I had still not come out to my parents or most family members or coworkers and was therefore still living a significant portion of my life hiding in *the closet*. I was involved in a new, serious relationship. I remember feeling overwhelmed by life, and it affected me both emotionally and physically.

I would talk to my partner and tell him about the recent hospitalization of my friend, what AIDS was doing to his body, and how much time the doctors said he had left – which was not much. I would talk about all this with great difficulty – like I had a tremendous lump in my throat. I found it difficult to speak – literally. So much so that I decided to go to the doctor and get my throat checked out to see what was going on. The next great journey of my life was about to begin.

I sat in the doctor's chair, opened my mouth, watched him put a mirrored instrument into the opening of my throat, and saw a puzzled expression come over his face. I did indeed have a lump in my throat. The mass was on my vocal cords and it was preventing them from vibrating, thus causing me to have difficulty speaking. He said it needed to be biopsied and that surgery would be required to do so. Mass, Surgery, Biopsy? I could hardly believe my ears as I sat there in the chair, listening to him.

"What was it?" I asked him.

"I don't know, it is quite irregular," he said.

He was an Ear, Nose and Throat (ENT) specialist, a surgeon even, with years of experience. He was a *specialist*, and he did not know what the mass was. Irregular? What did irregular mean?

Of course I was thinking of the C word, how could I not? I asked him if it could be cancer and he said he was uncertain, only the biopsy would determine for sure what it was.

Then he said, "I want you in surgery with me as soon as possible. I will biopsy the mass and then remove it from your vocal cord."

"Once you remove the mass, will my voice hoarseness go away?" I asked.

"Hopefully but I cannot give you any guarantees," he said. "Let's just go ahead and get the surgery scheduled so we can figure this out."

I walked out to the receptionist in a fog and she set the surgery up for that week.

After the surgery I awoke from the anesthesia and felt very ill with nausea. Then I felt the pain in my neck. Intense, biting pain – like an acute sore throat. My sister was sitting next to me in the recovery room. I attempted to say hello to her but no words came out. It became readily apparent, startlingly and stunningly apparent, that I was not able to speak.

The surgeon arrived to tell me what had happened during the surgery.

"I removed the mass from your vocal cords," he said.

"I am still not sure what it was, we will have to wait for the biopsy results. You will have to remain silent for the next seven days, so that your vocal cords can heal. I am giving you a pain medication prescription for the throat pain. I want to see you in my office next week."

Silent for seven days! – How would that be possible? Not sure what it was? – How could that be? What would I do at work? I had a demanding, vocally intensive job!

At the time, I was a Sales and Marketing director for a small start up firm. I spent the entire day using my voice – talking on the phone, making oral presentations and conducting meetings. I would have to contact my boss and let her know that I would need to use pen and paper to communicate for the next week until my voice returned.

As the ENT was walking out the door of my room he turned to me and said, "I want to reiterate how important it is that you do not speak for the next week. Vocal rest is very important for healing and the return of your speaking voice."

I eventually left the recovery room, drunk on pain medication, and my sister took me home. I lay down in my bed, popped another pain pill, and let the drugs carry me away from reality and into sleep.

Not being able to speak for the next week was excruciating. As I have said before, my voice was my lifeline in this world. I had developed a keen vocal ability that I used to deal with and manage all the negative aspects of my Complex whenever it would assert itself in my life – which was often. My voice was my buffer against my low self-esteem, not being good enough and inadequacy.

It turned out that my inability to speak was far more painful than the physical pain of the operation. I kept telling myself that it was only temporary, that in a week I would have my voice back and all would be fine.

I arrived at my ENT's office the next week filled with fear. What were the biopsy results? Did I have cancer? What would happen when I tried to speak?

"It is not cancer," the ENT said. I felt my world lighten. I felt the energy of relief forming in my feet and spreading, like an ocean wave, up through my body. A smile came to my face and I exhaled deeply. I could not help but notice, however, that there was no sign of happiness on the ENT's face.

"I am not sure what it is," he said. "It is not malignant, which is the good news, but the results are inconclusive as to exactly just what the mass was. I think it is safe to assume that it was just some sort of anomaly; a onetime occurrence. I will have you back in a couple of weeks just to monitor the situation and make sure all is well. Now, use your voice to say something to me."

I opened my mouth and attempted to speak to him. It was an experience that rocked me to my core. I could *barely* produce sound. The voice that came out was very hoarse, breathy and weak. It was shocking. He saw the astonishment on my face and said, "Okay, Okay, not too much. You need to still take it easy on your voice for a while. Speak only when you absolutely need to for the next two weeks until I see you again."

I left his office half filled with relief over not having cancer and half filled with dread over my lack of voice. Speak only when I absolutely need to. How was I going to do that? I need to speak all the time. In my job and in my social life – my voice defines me!

I made adjustments however I could. I convinced my boss that my voice would return soon, and I would be able to resume all my duties once it healed. I just had to be quiet for a while to let that healing occur. I curtailed my social life so that I wasn't tempted to speak. I motivated myself into speaking as little as possible by telling myself that by not speaking now I was ensuring the return of my voice later. The two weeks until my next ENT appointment seemed an eternity.

When I returned to see him I was filled with anxiety, as my vocal quality had not gotten any better. Why was my voice still hoarse and weak? Why did it descend into just a whisper after only minimal use – after just a few sentences spoken? Why was I not healing?

He once again placed the viewing mirror instrument deep into my throat and examined my vocal cords. He spent a lot of time looking; tears came to my eyes because it took everything I had not to gag on the instrument. Finally he removed it, and as he did I saw the look on his face. It was a look of concern. Bewilderment, actually. He paused in his chair, eyes gazed downward. I felt an old familiar force come over me as I sat in that examination chair – *dread*. I knew, at my core, that something was wrong.

He could not look at me as he said, "Well, I am sorry to say, I see additional masses on your vocal cords. These are new and were not there when I removed the original mass three weeks ago."

"What? New mass*es*, plural?? In just three weeks? What is this? What is happening?" were the whispered questions that flew out of my mouth.

"I am sorry, I just don't understand it," he said. "I have never seen anything like it. I am going to refer you to the Ear, Nose and Throat research center at the University of Washington (UW) Medical Center for examination. There are physicians there that specialize in rare conditions of the throat. I wish I could help you more, but I have reached the limit of my expertise. I will make a referral to get you in there right away."

"Will my vocal quality get better?" I asked.

"Probably not. Not with those new masses on your vocal cords. I would continue to rest your voice until we figure out what is going on."

I walked to the receptionist and she got me the next possible appointment, which was in a week's time.

I left the office, stunned. I walked out of the building and onto the sunny sidewalk. I felt short of breath, and I stopped and leaned up against the building to rest. Tears came to my eyes. I lowered my face into my hands and sobbed.

I had to tell work what was going on. There was no way to hide the fact that I could barely speak. No way to hide the fact that I could not do most of the tasks associated with my job. My boss agreed to make accommodations for another week, until my appointment at the University where I would hopefully find out what was going on with me.

I withdrew socially for the next week. I could not produce enough volume in my voice to be heard anywhere but the most quiet of locations. Restaurants, bars, parties, group events – the core places of my social life – were all too loud. I was motivated to not speak by the thought that if I rested my voice, it would be easier for the UW Medical Center doctors to diagnose my condition and cure me.

## Scope

The time for the appointment came, and I found myself standing outside the medical center building, staring at it. It was an enormous, grey colored concrete structure; stark and bleak in its appearance. Outside the main door was a sign emblazoned with big bold lettering – University of Washington Medical Center – Hospital and Research Facility. "Research Facility?" I thought to myself with questioning thoughts. Did I have a condition that was so unusual that I needed to go to a research facility for diagnosis?

With nervous worry, I passed through the doors and entered the building. I checked in at the Ear, Nose and Throat department, which here was called Otolayngology (I found it to be a frightening word) and was escorted to an examination room. I undressed and put on a hospital gown, as I had been instructed to do, and then looked around the room while waiting for the *Otolaryngological Surgeon*. There were all sorts of medical gadgets in the room; all were unfamiliar to me and they made me nervous. What was going to happen to me? What kind of examination was I in for? Which of these gadgets would be used on me?

The surgeon entered the room and introduced himself to me. He was tall, bearded and had a dark complexion. He said that he had reviewed my file and that he needed to take a look at my larynx.

"What is the larynx?" I asked. He described it to me as the hollow muscular organ forming the air passage to the lungs and holding the vocal cords; also known as the voice box.

"Have you ever had a laryngeal scope before?" he asked me.

A laryngeal scope? I thought to myself. Until two minutes ago I did not even know what the larynx was, never mind having it *scoped*.

"No," I replied.

He reached over and grabbed an instrument off of the wall. It consisted of a black handle in the shape of a tube, about 12 inches long and an inch and a half in diameter, which had several buttons and dials on it. Extending from the end of this tube was a long, slender, flexible, filament like cable. At the very end of the cable, at the tip, shone a small light.

"This instrument is called a laryngeal scope," he said. "It will allow me to see your larynx in great detail, including the masses that are in there. What I am going to do is place the tip of this scope (he pointed to the very end of the cable that contained the small light) into one of your nostrils. I am then going to feed the cable up into your nose, through your sinus cavities, down into your throat and into your larynx. There is a tiny camera at the end of this cable that will let me see your larynx, vocal cords and the masses. These controls (he pointed to the buttons and dials on the handle) will allow me to move the camera around once I get it into your larynx."

His description of what he was proposing to do to me struck fear into every aspect of my being. At least I would be under general anesthesia during the procedure, I thought. He must have seen the resulting look of desperation on my face, and so he continued.

"I am going to spray a numbing solution up into the nostrils of your nose which should help to deaden the gag reflex and some of the pain. I will need you to sit perfectly still in the examination chair and breathe easily as I work the scope down into your larynx."

Then it dawned on me, in startling, agonizing clarity – I was going to be awake during this procedure!

"I am going to be awake during this?!" I exclaimed.

He heard the fear in my voice and saw the bewildered expression on my face. He replied, "Yes, you have to be as I need you to speak and move your vocal cords while I am in there so I can get a complete picture of what is going on. I also need you to perform some breathing tasks while I am in there. You need to be awake to do this. I will use the numbing medication in your nose and that will help. I will go very slowly in order to create as little discomfort for you as possible. I am sorry that you have to go through this, but it is the only way to get the information we need to move forward with a diagnosis and treatment."

I knew I was sunk. There was no way to avoid it. I could not refuse this procedure and walk out of the hospital with undiagnosed, growing masses in my throat. I knew that I was in the hands of a talented specialist at a world renowned medical facility – an excuse for going elsewhere for better care and more expertise was not valid.

"Are you okay with moving ahead with this?" I heard him ask.

"I am very nervous," I said. "But, I don't feel as if I have a choice so let's proceed."

He looked at me in the eyes and very gently said, "I will be as gentle and careful as I can be."

He pushed a button on the wall and very soon his assistant appeared. The assistant would be helping hold me in place and keep me motionless while the surgeon worked the scope into me.

I felt the electricity of nervousness coursing through my body as the doctor raised an aerosol container to my nose, inserted it into the opening of my left nostril and sprayed the numbing medication into my nose. I felt a cold sting as the sour tasting medication worked its way up through my nose and down the back of my throat. He then did the same in my right nostril.

He then grabbed the laryngeal scope and placed a small dab of clear gel on the end of the cable, partially dimming the light at the tip.

"This lubricant gel will help the scope go in more easily," he said.

I watched in horror. As he prepared the instrument for use, I had time to think about what was actually happening to me. And boy, did my mind *think*. Thoughts in rapid fire succession, like a raging river, dragged me along: Why has this happened to me? Haven't I endured enough in this life already? Why me? Would I die? Was this some crazy fatal disease? How much pain was I about to be subjected to?

Like a freight train the thoughts came, seemingly unstoppable, until, with a force akin to Thor's hammer, the following words came crashing down on my thoughts, putting an abrupt end to them...

"Okay, we're ready," the surgeon said.

The assistant put his hand on my forearm – steadying me.

"I need you to remain as still as you possibly can and breathe slowly and regularly."

He raised the scope up to the level of my face and inserted the lighted end-tip of the cable into my right nostril.

I felt a tickle as the tip brushed by my nose hairs. "Wasn't I supposed to be numb?" I thought.

Then I felt a new, bizarre sensation. The sensation of something moving up in the back of my nose. A prick, mild at first, then a biting pain deep in the inner tissues of my nose. Startled, I lunged forward and instantly the assistant put pressure on my forearm. He reached out with the other hand, placed it on my shoulder and applied pressure, forcing me back against the chair. I winced and water came to my eyes. I then felt the cable sliding through my nose as the surgeon forced the tip of the scope deeper into me.

Another biting pain struck way back, deep in my sinuses. The assistant was ready this time, the strength of his hands and arms holding me firmly in place in the chair.

Then I felt a presence in the back of my throat. A tickle at first, then a piercing sensation as the tip of the scope bumped into tissue as it descended into my throat. A significant length of the cable was now stretched out within me and I could feel it sliding through the cavities of my head and neck.

"Breathe," said the surgeon. "Please breathe."

I realized that I had been holding my breath in defense against this onslaught. I exhaled fast and hard then inhaled deeply. As I did I could feel the entire scope move within me. It was an intensely foreign and unpleasant sensation. Then I felt a discomfort deep down in my throat.

"I am entering your larynx now," said the surgeon. "I want you to breathe slowly and easily."

This was no simple task. I was tight, tense, nervous and fearful. My body was rigid. These were not bodily conditions that were conducive to *breathing slowly and easily*. I tried to calm myself. Tried to do as he asked.

"Now I want you to swallow. There is some mucous on the tip of the scope that is interfering with the camera's view and I need you to swallow to clear it," the surgeon said.

It was at this point that I learned how many of the bodies muscles were involved in the act of swallowing. I attempted to swallow as he commanded, but I could not. The intrusion of the scope into my head and neck cavities had caused such a trauma, that my neck muscles had frozen – I could not swallow. It felt like the entirety of my head and neck had become immobilized.

"Breathe," said the surgeon. "Breathe, relax and swallow for me – you can do it!"

I took several labored breaths and attempted to swallow once again. Never had something so automatic, so easy, so autonomic – the simple act of swallowing – become so difficult, or conscious.

I summoned what seemed like everything I had in me and forced my body to swallow. I felt the wave of muscular action flow down through my face and neck and the physical act of swallowing took place. It seemed as if my muscles clamped around every part of the scope that was within me – I could feel every portion of it.

"Very good," the surgeon said. "Now I can see clearly."

He continued, "Now, I want you to take a deep breath and say 'eeeeee'." His voice created a high pitched *eeeeee* sound during his demonstration of the sound that he wanted me to create.

I inhaled and attempted to make the sound. As the muscles in my throat contracted and the *eeeeee* sound started to come out, I gagged. I gagged violently, which evolved into a deep convulsing cough. The surgeon recoiled and the assistant held me down. I felt a sour taste rise up in my throat and I felt nauseous, as if I were going to vomit.

"Breathe," said the surgeon, trying to calm me down. "When you are ready, try to make the *eeeeee* sound again."

I resisted the urge to vomit and focused on my breathing. I inhaled deeply and clenched down hard in an attempt to create the requested sound. Out came a slight, weak, *eeeeee* sound.

"Very good," he said.

There was a long pause as the surgeon manipulated the scope within me, examining my larynx, throat and trachea. I could feel the scope moving within me. The manipulations kept me on the edge of gagging and my body's strong twitching reactions were minimized by the firm stabilizing pressure applied by the assistant.

"Try again please," he said.

I inhaled deeply once again and produced another faint *eeeeee* sound.

## Vocal Cords

He continued with his examination by asking me to produce a series of different vocal sounds. Some I could produce, some I could not. It seemed as if the examination lasted for an eternity.

Finally he said, "Okay, now I am going to remove the scope. Please continue to breathe slowly and easily." In preparation for the removal, I felt the assistant apply additional pressure to my shoulder and forearm.

He removed the scope rapidly. I felt a burning sensation start in my throat and work its way up into my head and nose as the cable was being retracted. The tip of the scope came flying out of my nose, and I gasped. Then I coughed violently. Then I sneezed intensely. Mucous and lubricant projected forth from my nostrils, striking the lab coat of the surgeon – he recoiled. He quickly reached for tissues and passed me a handful. I applied the wad to my nose and mouth and closed my eyes.

I sat there, reeling from the experience. There was silence in the room as the surgeon and assistant remained quiet and still, allowing me some time to recover. Then, the doctor thanked the assistant, excused him, and he left the room.

### RRP

I wiped my water filled eyes and looked at the surgeon.

"You did a great job," he said. "I was able to get a really good look at your throat, larynx, vocal cords, and trachea." He continued, "I am sorry to say that you have several masses on your vocal cords and on the walls of your larynx. This is why you are having such difficulty speaking. I need to do surgery to remove the masses. The surgery will clear your airway and hopefully improve your speaking voice. I will take a biopsy of the masses during the surgery and run some tests so that we can determine, for sure, exactly what this is."

I was aghast. I just had surgery. Another one? Clear my airway? Hopefully improve my speaking voice? Determine exactly, what this is? Does he have any idea of what this is? My mind whirled.

I asked him, "Do you know what this is?"

"I will not know for certain until we run the tests, but I am quite sure that you have Recurrent Respiratory Papillomatosis (RRP). RRP is a rare disease of the respiratory tract in which tumors grow in the air passages leading from the nose and mouth into the lungs. Although the tumors can grow anywhere in the respiratory tract, their presence in the larynx causes the most frequent problems, as you are experiencing with your voice loss. The condition in the larynx is called, more specifically, laryngeal papillomatosis. The tumors may vary in size and grow very quickly. The tumors that you have look very much like RRP tumors."

Stunned in my chair, I managed to squeak out the one question that came, front and center, to my mind. "What is the cure?" I asked.

"I am sorry to say that there is no known cure. The treatment is to surgically remove the tumors so that your airway remains clear and you are able to breathe normally, and to improve your voice quality as much as possible."

"So once they are surgically removed I will get my voice back?" I asked.

"Your voice quality should improve, but we won't know how much until after the surgery and your recovery. I need to let you know that with RRP, the tumors often grow back even after having been removed."

"Are the tumors always benign?" I asked.

"With RRP, the tumors are usually benign, but there have been cases where they have metastasized into cancer," he replied. "We will have to watch you closely."

"Can they spread to other areas?" I asked.

"Yes," he said. "They can spread to other areas of the respiratory tract, including the lungs. We will work to make sure that does not happen to you."

"What caused this? How did I get it?" I asked.

"The tumors are caused by the human papilloma virus (HPV). HPV is very common and humans have much exposure to it. Generally the body is able to fight it off without a problem. Why the virus manifests itself in the respiratory tract of RRP patients is unknown. I see from your chart that you are a gay man and that you have recently been tested for HIV and you are negative, so we know that HIV is not a contributing factor."

I cannot overstate the level of anxiety that was building

in me as this conversation unfolded. The lingering pain in my head and neck cavities was combining with mental and emotional anguish; I felt like I was going to vomit.

The surgeon noticed my discomfort. He reached out and placed his hand over mine.

He looked me straight in the eyes and said, "I am very sorry. I want you to know that we will do everything we can for you and that you are in good hands here. I want you to work with my staff to schedule the surgery as soon as possible so that we can get your airway clear and biopsy the tissue to confirm the diagnosis. Is there someone here with you?"

"No, I came by myself," I replied.

He buzzed for his assistant.

"Do you have any further questions for me?" he asked.

"How do you perform the surgery," I replied. "Will I be under anesthesia?"

"Yes, you will be unconscious under general anesthesia. I will remove the tumors using a laser, cold steel instruments or a combination of the two depending on what I find in your larynx."

"What will the recovery be like?"

"You will need to refrain from speaking for several days after the surgery and then use your voice cautiously and minimally for two weeks to a month. I will give you a better idea of this after the surgery," he replied. "We will get you into professional voice therapy after your recovery."

The assistant entered the examination room. The surgeon instructed the assistant to take me to the surgery scheduling desk and get me set up for surgery as soon as possible.

The surgeon reached out and shook my hand. He said, "I will see you soon. If you think of any more questions between now and the surgery, please call the office and we will address them for you."

I thanked him and then followed the assistant out the door of the examination room. I was in a smoky daze as we walked down the hallway and arrived at the surgery scheduling desk. The assistant told the scheduler that I need to be set up for a *direct laryngoscopy* surgical procedure as soon as possible. There happened to be a cancellation in the surgery schedule for the next morning, so I was scheduled then.

I was instructed to not eat anything after 8:00 pm that evening. I was told to not take any medications of any kind. I was told to be at the hospital at 7:00 am the following morning.

It all happened so very quickly. Soon, I had an informational surgery packet in my hand and was heading out the door of the hospital. I had no time to process what had just happened to me, until I reached the light of day in the courtyard outside the facility. There, I turned and began to walk to my car, parked a few blocks away. As I walked I reviewed in my mind everything that had just happened in the last hour and a half of my life. The following words became imbedded in my mind and struck fear deep in my core: disease, tumors, surgery, incurable, recurring, virus, cancer, voice loss, RRP.

## Will I get my voice back?

I called my boss and told her what was happening and that I would not be at work for the next several days. I did not tell her about the duration of the voice loss that was to come, because I did not know how to respond to the inevitable question, "How will you perform your job if you can't speak?"

That night I told my boyfriend, my friend who was dying from AIDS, my sister and my parents what was going on. My mother asked if I wanted her to come out for the surgery. I said no as it was scheduled for early tomorrow morning and there was no way that she could get to Seattle from New Hampshire in time – which was the truth. The real motivation behind me telling her not to come, however, was the fear that she might discover that I was gay.

With such short notice, there was no one available to accompany me to the surgery. The next morning, I left my apartment at 6:15 am and took the bus to the hospital. Unable to eat or drink for breakfast, I was hungry and thirsty and had a splitting headache. I walked into the hospital, checked in at the surgery center desk and was escorted to the surgery preparation center. The room was aseptic and cold. Gleaming tile floors and walls, bright fluorescent overhead lights, polished metal instrument and apparatus surfaces, and monotone colors, lent a feel of sterility.

I was told to change into my hospital gown attire and wait for the nurse to administer my IV. I complied. I felt cold and raw as the thin, course material of the gown enveloped my body. I applied the bulbous, fine mesh hat to my head and the tight, scratchy booties to my feet. I sat down on the hospital bed that had been designated for my use. As I did I heard the crumpling, crunching sound of a bed that was being protected by a plastic under sheet. It all felt stiff and forbidding.

As I sat there, I experienced the sounds of the surgery prep center; the beeping and pinging of electronic medical devices, cautious voices of nurses and surgeons explaining procedures, nervous and anxious voices of patients anticipating surgeries, the squeak of arms of hospital beds being raised and lowered. Then the sights: gurneys passing by laden with patients and bags filled with dripping fluids, medical staff dressed in sterile surgery garb intently focused on reading the charts in their hands, medical devices flashing their warning lights.

My body felt consumed by a surly concoction of lack of food and water, trepidation and bewilderment. I felt as if I was on the verge of collapse when the nurse appeared and introduced herself. She took a good look at me and, sensing my discomfort said, "I am going to administer your IV. Once I do, we will give you something that will allow you to relax."

She prepared my forearm for the insertion of the IV needle. "Your veins have kinda disappeared," she said. "That happens when you are nervous, so please try to relax."

She placed the long white IV needle next to my skin, the insertion point on top of a faint vein. She tipped the needle up, pushed it forward and the tip penetrated my skin. I felt a sharp pain as the needle entered my forearm. Blood squirted out from the insertion point.

"Darn," said the nurse, gently and under her breath.

"What is wrong?" I asked.

"Your veins are being squirrely. I am going to have to try again."

She had missed the vein. She pulled the long needle out of my tissue. As she did I winced from the pain of the lengthy needle being dragged through the muscle of my forearm. Blood oozed from the hole in my skin and I felt nauseous.

Noticing my discomfort, she said, "Please breathe deeply and try to relax."

She bandaged the hole in my arm to stop the bleeding, prepared a new IV needle and then proceeded to knead my forearm in search of another vein. This time she found a larger one, at my wrist next to my hand. She inserted the needle and successfully threaded the vein. I flinched from the pain as the long needle penetrated my wrist.

I felt assaulted. Not just from the insertion of the IV, but from the cumulative effect of everything that was happening to me. I was lightheaded, nauseous and full of dread. The stress must have been evident on my face as the nurse looked at me and said, "The IV is in now. I will get the anesthesiologist, and he will give you something to relax."

She walked away from my bed and as she did, she pulled a floor to ceiling curtain around my area, giving me privacy and isolating me from the rest of the surgery prep center. I lay there alone. My head was throbbing, my stomach was queasy and my forearm hurt. But all of these physical symptoms paled in comparison to what was going on in my mind. My thoughts and emotions were raging, fueled by a lifetime of anxiety and by a Complex that was fully activated. I lay there, motionless, alone and lost in it all; consumed and overpowered.

I was startled back into the present moment by the *szuuuut* sound of the curtain being pulled aside. The anesthesiologist appeared in the opening and introduced himself. He asked me numerous questions about my general health and I answered him with my thin, weak, breathy voice. He told me that he would be putting me to sleep using general anesthesia drugs, and he would be monitoring me during the time that I was under.

He then said, "I am going to give you a drug now called Versed. It will relax you before going into the surgery room." He took a syringe from the pocket of his white lab coat, removed the cover from the needle and inserted the needle into an orifice in the IV tube that led to my wrist. He said, "I will see you soon in the OR," and then left my space and drew the curtain closed.

Alone once again, my mind began to reel with thought. I was on the verge of being lost in my head, once again, when it hit. The Versed had worked its way through the IV and into my bloodstream. It struck me in one fell swoop, like a see through veiled curtain being drawn across my thinking mind – suppressing it. I felt a calmness come over me, as my thinking diminished. I was still completely aware of my surrounding and what was going on, but I was experiencing reality as if peering through a fog. Anxiety seemed to melt away.

*Szuuuut* went the opening curtain as the nurse appeared. "Time to go," she said. She released the locks on the wheels of my hospital bed, gave it a push and we began to move out of the surgery prep center. We entered the hallway and rolled down to the end. We stopped at a large closed door that was labeled Surgery Room 4. She hit a circular button at the side of the door, and it opened with a swooshing sound. I felt a rush of cold air emanate from the room and fall across me; surgery rooms are kept cold to inhibit germs. The nurse pushed my bed into the room. Apparatuses were everywhere; giant light mechanisms hanging from the ceiling, dials and meters and electronic readouts, a surgery table appearing like an octopus with tentacles of cables emanating from all corners, armlike devices hanging from the ceiling. There were numerous people in the room; surgery staff milling around preparing for my procedure. In my *relaxed* state under the influence of Versed, it seemed like I had entered a fantasy world. One that was foreign and foreboding.

My hospital bed was aligned parallel and immediately next to the surgery table, and I was asked by the nurse to transfer my body from the bed to the table. As I attempted to move my body I experienced a new aspect of the Versed. I was slow to move, lethargic and unsteady. I felt several hands grasp me as the surgery staff moved in to steady me and support my body as I moved.

I transferred myself to the surgery table and came to rest in a sitting up position. The nurse approached me and said, "Nice job, now lie down please."

I could not lie down. Even the calming effects of the Versed could not stop fear from rising up within me. I conjured an image in my mind of tumors in my throat and a laser beam cutting me. Words flooded my brain: disease, tumors, surgery, incurable, recurring, virus, cancer, voice loss, RRP. I envisioned not waking up. The time for the surgery was now, and I freaked.

The staff noticed this and they all gathered around me. The anesthesiologist placed his hand on my shoulder and told me that everything was going to be okay. He said I am going to give you a little more Versed to help you relax. He thrust another syringe into the orifice of my IV. "Please lie down," he said, and I felt the pressure of his hand on my shoulder gently forcing me down.

Just as I became flat on my back the surgeon appeared and said hello to me. I looked up at him and asked him to describe what he was going to do to me. He described the surgical procedure as follows, "Once you are sound asleep we will position your head so that your mouth and airway are as open as they can be. I will then insert the laser beam instrument into your mouth, down your throat and into your larynx. I will then work the laser to remove the tumors."

Through the veil of Versed, I felt dread.

At that very moment the second dosage of the drug kicked in. I felt a heavier curtain descend across my being and consciousness.

Realizing that I was losing control and this nightmare was about to commence, I looked at the anesthesiologist and said, "Please let me know when you start to put me to sleep!"

"Okay," he said. Realizing that I was starting to freak out a little, he placed a hand on my shoulder and in a soft voice said, "I am starting to put you to sleep now." As he said the words, a clear plastic mask appeared in front of my face and descended toward my nose and mouth. It was an ominous looking device, with many tubes radiating from it. My mind concocted the image of an octopus latching onto my nose and mouth, trying to suffocate me. My body startled with a jerk as the mask made contact with my face. The surgery staff responded with many hands descending onto my body, holding me in place.

"Please breathe normally, and silently count back from 100," said the anesthesiologist.

I began the count in my mind – 100, 99, 98. The lights overhead increased in intensity as the surgery staff continued their prep work. For some unknown reason, I raised my left arm and made the waving motion to the staff, as if waving goodbye. I remember the smile on the nurse's face as she pushed my arm back down on the bed.

97, 96, 95 ... for just a fleeting instant, I felt the process of losing consciousness. The complete and total loss of control, the fear of not waking up, the wondering of what would happen to me while I was unaware – all this danced through my head until, with dramatic certainty, the dark curtain descended, and I crossed the border into unconsciousness.

The first thing I remember upon waking up was sharp, throbbing pain deep in my throat. Just partially conscious, I instinctively swallowed as if to clear my throat and as I did, a searing, voluminous pain radiated through my neck and head. It startled me into a more complete consciousness, and I realized that I was alive and that I had made it through the surgery. The intensity of the pain was unexpected and made me realize that something significant had happened in my larynx. I found myself alone in a space surrounded on three sides by curtains, the fourth side open to the nurses' station. I was in a hospital bed hooked up to an IV. Without thinking and in response to discomfort in my throat, I swallowed again. The pain once again radiated through my neck and head. My body coughed in response, and I convulsed from the pain.

A recovery room nurse heard my cough and, realizing that I was awake, came over to my bed. She said, "Hi there, how are you doing?"

Instinctively, I opened my mouth to speak with the intention of saying, "My throat really hurts." But nothing came out! My attempt at producing voice was met by excruciating pain radiating from my throat and my face crumpled in a wince. No words came out – it startled me to my core.

The nurse responded, "Oh, that's right, you can't talk. How is your pain level? Just hold up your fingers indicating 1 through 10, with 10 being the worst pain."

I held up eight fingers. She said, "Oh, let me get you some pain medication then," and off she went. She returned quickly with a syringe that she emptied into my IV. "That should reduce the pain," she said. "The surgeon should be here soon to talk to you about the results of the procedure. Just rest and relax for now."

I lay there in my bed – terrified. I was in intense pain, and I had not been able to speak when I tried to. Still groggy from the anesthesia, I closed my eyes. The pain medication kicked in, took the sharp bite out of the pain, but much discomfort remained.

A significant amount of time passed before the surgeon appeared. When he finally did, I was back to full consciousness. He greeted me and then described what happened during the surgery.

"Well, I am sorry to say that you had multiple tumors in your larynx and on your vocal cords. I am quite certain that they were papilloma tumors, but I sent a sample off to the lab anyway, just to get confirmation. I was able to remove all of them with the laser, which is good news. How is your pain level?"

Afraid to speak, I held up eight fingers.

"Ah," he said. "That makes sense; I had to do a lot of work in there which is what is causing that level of pain for you. I will make sure that you get strong pain medication and have some to take home with you."

"I want you to try and speak for me. Can you say the words Many More Mom, please?"

I hesitated, knowing the pain that I was going to experience when I tried to talk. I opened my mouth and attempted to voice the words Many More Mom. The pain was not as intense as before, clearly the pain medication was helping. No voice came out, however. Just a faint whisper of the words Many More Mom came out of my mouth.

The surgeon responded by saying, "That makes sense. Your lack of voice is due to the work I had to do to remove the tumors from your vocal cords. You will need to remain silent for the next several days and rest your voice for the next two weeks in order to get some voice back."

I felt the look of horror come over my face as my mouth opened with a silent gasp in response to this news. The surgeon saw my response, put his hand on top of mine and said, "I am sorry. I know this is difficult. I want you to schedule a follow up appointment with me in one week's time so that I can evaluate your recovery process. Do you have any questions for me?"

I nodded yes. Knowing that I was unable to speak, he turned to the nurse and said, "Can you please bring me a pad of paper and pen?"

The nurse responded and handed the items to me. I can

remember, like it was five minutes ago, what the first question was that came to my mind. It was the first question that I would write on the pad.

I wrote on the paper – Will I get my voice back? I then turned the pad of paper around and showed it to him.

He read the question, hesitated and turned his head to the side – thinking. I shall never forget his body language. Without him uttering a word, I knew that he did not have a definitive answer to this question. I knew that there would be no response such as, "Of course. Your voice will be good as new once you heal up." Or, "Sure, all looks great and you can expect a full recovery."

Instead, after his hesitation, he turned to me and said, "You will get *some* voice back. Just how much I am not certain. It depends upon how your vocal cords heal and how the disease progresses. We will know more in time, and my staff and I will work with you to help you."

I quickly scribbled on the paper - What do you mean by, "How the disease progresses?"

"Based on the number of papilloma tumors in your larynx, your disease is quite aggressive. As I mentioned to you before, papilloma tumors have a tendency to reoccur and we have no known way of stopping them from growing. Ultimately, only time will tell us how much of your voice returns. I will work with you, along with a speech therapist, to give you the best voice quality possible."

Frantically, I wrote down my next question. "What

about my job? I have a very vocally intensive job. Can I still do it?"

"I would recommend not. Based on what is going on here, you should no longer do anything that requires a lot of speaking. I am happy to write you a doctor's note to excuse you from your vocal duties for at least the next couple of weeks. I am sorry, I know that this is all very difficult to hear, but I think that you should try to find employment now that does not rely on your speaking voice."

The surgeon asked me if I had any questions, I nodded no, and he dismissed himself. The nurse removed my IV, told me I could get dressed whenever I felt like it and departed. As I lifted my head from the pillow I felt a shot of pain move through my neck; clearly, head and neck movements were going to be uncomfortable for a while. I got dressed, slightly unstable and still groggy from the anesthesia, and walked to the nurses' station. The nurse handed me my pain medication and as she did, my boyfriend appeared to take me home. I wrote - Hi, I can't talk for a while, to him on the notepad. The nurse explained the situation to him and he nodded his understanding to her and me. We walked out of the recovery room – in silence.

## Many, My, Mom

On the ride home my mind was still numb from the anesthesia, and it processed very little. My boyfriend dropped me off at my apartment; I crawled into bed and fell asleep. When I awoke I was clear-headed as the anesthesia had completely worn off. So had the pain medication – my throat burned. I quickly took a pain pill, sat down on the couch and began to process the day's events. I was bewildered by what was happening to me. I realized that I had to tell my boss that I could no longer do my job and that was terrifying. I realized that I could no longer do any job that relied on my voice. "What job didn't rely on the voice," I thought to myself. How was I going to support myself? I needed to apply for disability, I thought. Disability, me? – How humiliating! My mind whirled with doomsday scenarios, until the pain medication kicked in, and everything went dull. The pain medication provided not only relief from the discomfort in my throat, but from the agony of my overactive thinking mind. I remember thinking to myself, so this is why people get addicted to this stuff. I fell into mindless TV watching for the rest of the evening.

The next seven days, until my follow-up appointment with the surgeon, gave me my first real experience with voicelessness. It was relentlessly frustrating. My voice had become my primary tool for dealing with my life. It was my strongest ally and my most powerful defense mechanism. Having it totally stripped away, as it was for these seven days, brought me to the old *Leslie the Faggot* place of helplessness and despair that I had experienced in my youth. I was not conscious of it at the time, but the voicelessness was the most powerful Complex activator that I had ever experienced. My mind churned with negative thoughts which produced the associated negative emotions, and those emotions grew in strength. It became crippling. All I could do was think of the upcoming surgeon's appointment and the resulting approval to go ahead and speak once again. Pain pills and sleep were my defenses and they provided my only sanctuary until the day of the appointment.

I walked into the surgeon's office, eager with anticipation about being able to speak again. I had done my job; I had not spoken for a week. I felt strongly that if I did not speak, that my voice would heal well – it had been a powerful motivator to not open my mouth.

The surgeon greeted me and I nodded my hello, still remaining silent.

"Well, let's hear you say something now," he said. "I want you to say the words Many, My, Mom."

I opened my mouth and vocalized the words as he had requested.

"Many, My, Mom," I said. It was shocking. The voice that came out was weak, breathy and thin – not much more than a whisper.

Determined, I decided to try again and this time I pushed much harder. I could feel the muscles in my throat contract as I once again said, "Many, My, Mom."

The result was the same. I became terrified as I realized that my voice had not returned.

"Okay, that's enough," the surgeon said. He placed his hand on my forearm and said to me, "I am sorry to tell you, but I got the lab results back and you do have RRP. The tumors in your larynx are laryngeal papillomas."

His words fell over me like a rain of cement. I felt a

heaviness form in the pit of my stomach and radiate out into my body. Two words came front and center to my mind – incurable, recurring.

"Let's take a look inside," the surgeon said.

The dark cloud of dread came over me as I realized what his words meant – The Scope! He was going to feed the laryngeal scope down into my larynx and take a look. He buzzed for his assistant as he removed the instrument from the wall.

In a complete reenactment of what had happened before, I was lead through the scoping procedure: the assistant held me down, medication was sprayed in my nostrils, the scope was fed through my head and neck cavities and I was asked to produce various vocal sounds. All of it painfully uncomfortable.

The surgeon pulled the scope out of my head, gave me a minute to recover, looked at me and said, "During the surgery I had to do a lot of work in there to remove the tumors, and it is taking a while for your larynx and vocal cords to heal. The tissues in there are still quite red and inflamed. This is why your voice has not come back. You can talk now, but I want you to keep your voice use to a minimum. When you do use your voice, I want it to be only in quiet places where you do not have to raise or project your voice in order to communicate. In order for your vocal cords to heal, you need to be very careful about how and how much you use your voice. To help you, I am going to set up an appointment for you with a colleague of mine who is a voice therapist. She will teach you how to use your voice in a way that will not cause further damage to your vocal cords."

"Will you write a letter for me to my boss, in support of a disability claim at work?" I croaked in words that were barely more than a whisper.

"Absolutely," he said. "You should no longer be doing your vocally intensive job," he exclaimed.

"I want to see you in a month, in the interim, please work with my assistant to set up your voice therapy appointment."

I set up both appointments, got the disability support letter from my surgeon and left the hospital. I went to my work office, broke the news to my boss, handed her the disability support letter and spent the rest of the afternoon filing out the disability paperwork. I cleaned out my office, said goodbye to my coworkers and closed the door on my position as Director of Sales and Marketing.

I went to a local gay bar and ordered a drink. I needed relief desperately, and my hope was that it would come in the form of alcohol. In the bar, I had my first direct experience as to how my new disability would be affecting another area of my world – my social life. Bars are loud. This one was no exception. In the past I had always enjoyed the sounds of the music and voice chatter. Now the noise was a hindrance to communication. When I opened my mouth to order a drink, the bartender could not hear my weak voice over the noise of the bar. I grabbed a piece of paper and a pen, wrote down my drink order and handed it to the bartender. I sat there, consuming drink after drink, unable to talk to anyone. It was an intensely isolating feeling. The traumatic events of the day, in combination with the effects of the alcohol, activated my Complex and my mind began to produce its toxic thoughts. The combination of the alcohol and the depression rendered me insentient. I do not remember how I got home that evening.

# The Crux

## The Parting of the Waters

The next day I got a call alerting me to the fact that my friend with AIDS had been admitted to the hospital. Out of work now, I was free to go see him immediately. I arrived at the hospital and was directed to the *AIDS Ward*. Entering the ward on the ninth floor of the hospital was like entering a death factory. The smells of medicine and illness permeated the hallway. As I walked by each patient room, I could see what was left of human beings as they succumbed to the disease; emaciated bodies, sunken eyes, disease-ridden skin.

I entered my friend's room and was shocked by what I saw. I had seen him just two weeks ago, and the difference between then and now was staggering. His eyes were yellow; his skin thin and bruised, and his dramatic weight loss was undeniable. His cheeks were sunken, his breathing labored and his body trembled. He was hooked up to a staggering number of tubes leading into three different IV's. In an instant I knew that the end was near. This is what AIDS did to people – an astoundingly grisly and savage death. He turned his head to look at me, and a weak smile came across his face.

Before I could utter a word he said to me, "It is happening," referring to his descent into death. "My doctor says that there is nothing else that can be done. Can you please close the door – I need to talk to you."

The directness of his remarks startled me and all I could say was "Sure," as I got up and closed the door.

"I need to tell you what I did last week as I got my affairs in order. There is something I need you to do for me," he uttered as tears welled up in his eyes.

Before he could speak another word I rose up, threw my arms around his head and shoulders and hugged him. I began to cry, as did he. I could not speak, not just because the emotions made it difficult to do so, but also because my vocal cords were so compromised from RRP and the recent surgery. What typically for me would have been a time of vocalization – my voice used as a defense mechanism against what was happening – was instead a time of silent embracing. It was tremendously uncomfortable and remarkably cathartic all at the same time.

He began to cough which broke our embrace. He coughed violently and began to convulse from it. I became alarmed and asked, "Should I get somebody?"

He shook his head and waved his hand indicating no, and coughed out, "Wait just a minute."

I sat there, watching the spectacle in front of me. I saw my wonderful friend, so strong, vibrant and alive just a few months ago, now reduced to a retching, shuddering heap of bodily decay.

In what seemed like an interminable amount of time, his body finally calmed down to the point where he could speak again.

"Sorry about that," he said, and reached out and held my hand.

"I finished my will last week and in it there are instructions for you. I would like you to take my ashes and spread them out at *The Parting of the Waters*, in the Teton Wilderness Area in Wyoming, near the border of Yellowstone National Park. I have provided money in my will to cover expenses associated with hiring a horse-pack wilderness guide service to take you to there. It is many miles and several days travel by horse to get there and the guide service will be able to provision, accompany and guide you for the entire trip."

"My God," I said to him, holding back more tears. "What an incredibly appropriate place to memorialize your life. Tell me more about *The Parting of the Waters*."

"A stream called North Two Ocean Creek flows down from its drainage on the side of Two Ocean Plateau at the Continental Divide. A geologic formation in the drainage causes the creek to split its waters in two, more-or-less equally, and thus creates two new creeks called Pacific Creek and Atlantic Creek. From this split, North Two Ocean Creek waters flow either 3,500 miles to the Atlantic Ocean via Atlantic Creek and the Yellowstone, Missouri and Mississippi Rivers, or 1,400 miles to the Pacific Ocean via Pacific Creek and the Snake and Columbia Rivers. The place where North Two Ocean Creek splits in two is called

*The Parting of the Waters* and that is where I would like you to spread my ashes."

I shook my head at him with wonderment and amazement. "This incorporates your love of the mountains and the Yellowstone ecosystem, with your two homes – Missouri and Washington State. The Mississippi flows by your childhood Missouri home and the Columbia flows by your current Washington home," I said.

"Yes," he said, with a momentary light in his otherwise dark eyes. "It is a place that I have always wanted to go myself, but obviously, I will never make it. Will you please take me there; spread my ashes?"

I was overwhelmed by a powerful emotional cocktail of grief, joy, mourning, privilege, excitement and dread. What an honor it was to be asked by him to do such a noble thing for him. How exceptional of him to give such a profoundly spiritual gift. How tremendously sad that my friend whom I had shared so many beautiful mountain moments with would not be able to experience this place called *The Parting of the Waters*.

With a very subdued, barely audible voice I said to him, "Of course. It would be an honor. There is nothing that I would rather do, and I promise you that I will make it happen."

"That is so awesome," he replied. "Thank you! I brought a map of *The Parting of the Waters* area, and it is over there in my bag. Want to take a look at it?"

"Sure," I responded. We had always loved looking at

mountain topographic maps together; planning trips and envisioning adventures. I brought the map over to his bed, pulled up a chair and we unfolded it in his lap. We got lost in it, exploring the trails and the terrain and finding the exact spot where the waters of North Two Ocean Creek split. A lightness came into the room that had not been there before. For a short time, we forgot about the reality of the situation and got lost in our passion. It would be the last time that we would do so together. He soon began to fatigue, his eyes grew heavy and he fell asleep. I sat next to him, hesitant to fold up the map fearing the crinkling sound of the paper might awaken him. Much more powerful was the fear that this was the last time that we would be together.

The next night I got a call from the executor of his estate telling me that he had just died. I called a mutual friend, and we travelled to the hospital together. When we got to the AIDS Ward we were told that his body had already been quarantined and removed from the hospital – standard procedure for an HIV infected body. We greeted and consoled his sister, the only family member that came for the end, and then the executor handed me the map of *The Parting of the Waters* and said, "He wanted you to have this." She went on to say, "I will make arrangements to have the ashes transferred to you once they are available."

We said goodbye to the sister and the executor, and it was finished – just like that. No memorial service, no funeral, no celebration of life dinner, no family gathering – nothing. A life – invaded physically, emotionally, mentally and socially by a devastating and misunderstood disease – just disappeared.

We exited the hospital and entered the darkness of the outside night, neither one of us speaking, both of us processing the death. The AIDS epidemic had been a defining element of our young gay lives and here it was, front and center, giving us its most dramatic expression – the death of a loved one. And not just any kind of death, but a death surrounded with suspicion, fear, rejection, and all the other intensely negative social stigmas that were associated with AIDS at the time.

As my mind thought revolved into a spinning mass of thick sorrow and dread, I became unstable on my feet and moved to sit on a cement planter that was on the side of the hospital building. The emotion overflowed and I began to cry. The deep sorrow I felt was broken by an awareness that no sound came out when I cried. My vocal cords were no longer capable of producing the sounds associated with crying. It felt like a plug in me, not allowing the emotion to escape.

My friend put his arm around me, and we sat there in silence, for the longest time, our static finally broken by the cold night air seeping into our sorrowful bones. I had the map in my hand and looked at it. "I promise," I said under my breath, and we got up and headed home.

## The Tipping Point

I returned to my apartment to find a message on my answering machine from my parents. They wanted to come for a visit next month. This news was more than I could handle. I had still not come out to my parents, not shared with them my friend's death from AIDS, or any other aspect of my life that concerned my gayness – which was most of my life. I was still playing the devastating game of hiding, covering and veiling my life to shield them from the truth of who I was. Despite the difficulty that was involved with maintaining my charade, that difficulty was still overcome by the fear of discovery. The fear of their rejection, disapproval, disappointment – the fear of not being good enough. Their visit would require that I summon the energy to organize my life in such a way that they would not discover the truth while they were here. It took a tremendous amount of work to accomplish this and, with everything that was going on with me, the task seemed daunting.

I returned the call and continued the deceit. The first part of the call was an update on RRP, why my voice was so hoarse and weak and why I could not talk long because of it. I then told them that I would *love* to have them come to visit, lying through my teeth, but that they should wait a while as my vocal cords would have more time to heal and my speaking voice more time to improve. They reluctantly agreed to postpone the visit until summer. I hung up the phone with a tremendous sense of relief, knowing that I had bought myself some time.

My boyfriend and I had been invited out on my friend's boat to celebrate the opening day of boating season in Seattle. Opening day was a city-wide celebration, held every year in early May, to mark the beginning of the boating season. My friend had a big, beautiful, fully restored forty-two foot Chris Craft cabin cruiser. I was excited about the invite and the day, which had the potential to be very enjoyable. Swimming, boating, drinking, frolicking, socializing – a day on the water was so much fun, and *fun* was what I needed now more than anything.

The day of the invite dawned sunny and clear – a perfect day to be on a boat and participate in all the opening day festivities. The events of the day would include a boat parade through the Montlake Cut waterway, crew boat races, and participation in the log boom. The log boom would be comprised of a series of floating logs strung end to end and anchored in the water. Boats would tie up to the boom, side by side, making a continuous bridge of boats across the water. It would create an intoxicating social scene as people would hop from boat to boat, visiting, sharing food and drink and carousing. Music would blare from everywhere.

I was eager with excitement and anticipation as we walked onto the dock toward the boat. We were some of the last to arrive; the boat was crowded with people. My friend had upbeat Samba music blaring from the boat's audio system and people were already dancing, frolicking and socializing. We stepped across the gunwale and onto the Chris Craft. I was immediately confronted by a group of friends who reached out to greet and embrace me as I entered the boat. Instinctively, I opened my mouth to speak – forgetting. My weak voice could not be heard above the sounds emanating from the boat; people talking, music playing, engines humming in their warm up. "What was that you said? I could not hear you. What happened to your voice?" were the question that came in an instant. They could not hear my replies. My boyfriend came to my rescue and told them that I had recently had surgery on my throat and could not talk. Everyone expressed concern, asking if I was okay. My boyfriend continued to respond to their questions while they looked at me with concern and discomfort on their faces.

As the engine noise increased and the boat pulled away from the dock, I realized that I had not brought a pad and pen with me. I had no way to directly communicate. I realized, with horror, that I would be on this loud boat for the next several hours with no way to verbally communicate with anyone. I felt the deep well of dread activate inside me.

As we made our way through the boat, my boyfriend continued to act as the intermediary, explaining my situation to friends and strangers alike. It was devastating for me. My tool for managing and participating in life, my voice, was completely unavailable in this environment. I could not put on my vocal show, could not impress, and could not maintain my social image. It was humiliating for me. Painfully humiliating. I began to feel isolated. I began to feel *really* not good enough and my Complex activated. I headed for the bar in the hopes of getting some relief via alcohol. One drink led to another. I tried to find a place on the boat where there were no people, and I could just be by myself, but no such place existed – the boat was just too crowded.

As people engaged me in social conversation, I made a slashing motion across my throat indicating that I could not talk. Comments abounded: "Oh my god, you poor thing, I would never be able to not talk." "Your boyfriend must *love* it!" "I wish *my* boyfriend would just shut up like that." "What happened to your voice? – oh, that's right you can't talk – ha ha!"

And then I realized the harshest reality yet with regard to being unable to communicate vocally. Once people had an understanding of my condition and had made their various comments, they would be done with me. My lack of response and therefore lack of input into the conversation would cause their attention to drift back toward speaking people, who offered more substantive and entertaining interaction. I was left just standing there, awkward in my presence. I found that I could just drift back and away from the people that I had had the interaction with, and no one would notice. It was devastatingly painful for me.

One drink followed the next. I stood in a spot, leaning up against the side of the boat and observed in silence. No one noticed me. All I wanted to do was get off of that boat. To run, as fast as I could, from the intense pain that I was feeling inside and that was being generated as a result of this situation. But I could not run. I was on a boat in the middle of a large lake, I was trapped. My boyfriend had left my side to mix and mingle with friends and participate in social conversation. I watched him talking. I watched all of them – talking. I had a deep and profound realization of how central to human existence is the speaking voice. The voice connects us, expresses us, and allows us to present ourselves to the world. It is a defining human characteristic that creates intense bonds.

As I stood there, observing and realizing all this, my mind brought forth the words of the surgeon – tumors, recurring, incurable, voice loss, RRP. The devastating mental and emotional aspects of my fully engaged Complex descended deeper into me. At that moment, the results of losing my voice due to RRP became indelibly clear in my mutilated mind. I was even *more* defective than before; more inadequate, more incapable and more unable than *ever* before – the onslaught strengthened and deepened my Complex. I really was *Leslie the Faggot*.

And there was no escape. For the next several hours I remained in this state of agony, negotiating the boat in a way that caused me to interact with as few people as possible. What was supposed to be a day of bliss in a joyous setting had turned into the biggest nightmare that I could have possibly imagined. My boyfriend could tell that there was something unsettled going on in me, and he came by occasionally to check on me. I could not share my distress with him of course, because I could not communicate vocally with him either. Knowing what was going on with me more than anyone, he said to me, "It must be difficult to be on this boat and unable to talk with anyone." It was the understatement of the century and his words brought me to the brink of emotional collapse. My eyes watered up. The only thing that kept me from a total emotional breakdown was the fear of the humiliation that such a scene would produce on that crowded boat. He saw the tears in my eyes and stayed with me for a while. After a time, when it appeared that I had calmed down, he asked if I minded if he went and talked to a friend that he had spied in the crowd. I nodded my approval and away he went. I watched him move across the boat, greet his friend and they erupted into conversation and laughter. Unable to bear the scene, I turned away and gazed out across the sea of boats and water activities that were going on all around us. The tears returned to my eyes.

The interminably long day finally came towards a close as the boat returned to its home dock. I positioned myself as the first person to disembark and made a hand gesture toward my boyfriend indicating that I would meet him out on the dock. I also waved an expansive wave toward the captain of the boat in order to get his attention. Once he saw me I blew a kiss of thank you, feeling obligated to do so even though not one tiny aspect of my being was grateful for the experience that I had just endured.

I met my boyfriend back at the car. He was in a jovial, spirited mood – clearly the result of what had been a very enjoyable day on the water for him. On the drive home he was very talkative, recounting the day's activities to me, recreating all of their pleasurable aspects in his mind as he spoke. I sat there listening, the contrast between his day and mine becoming sharper and sharper. My mind seized on the contrast, and it took me further into despair. After a time, he put his hand on my knee and asked me if I was okay. All I could muster was a hoarse, breathy and weak, "Yeah," audible now that we were in the quiet of the car. I did not have the energy to produce any greater response. The events of the day had been such a prolonged attack that my reserves were completely spent. There was a deep numbness in me. Strangely, it seemed like the numbness was acting like a cap or a plug over something that was heaving inside of me. Something that I could not access, yet I knew was there.

The numbness-capped heaving continued as we walked

up the stairs to the apartment. Once inside, my boyfriend played a new message that had been recorded on the answering machine. It was an invite to a party that evening. The invite was from a friend that had been on the boat during the day. The *Opening Day of Boating Season* festivities would be continuing into the night at this party, and we were invited.

"Wanna go?" said my boyfriend. My mind had already shifted into anxiety mode and before I could respond the thoughts came – another party, lots of people talking, loud music, unable to talk, unable to communicate, not good enough, humiliation, isolation.

I could not form any words. I looked at my boyfriend. I can remember feeling what my face must have looked like – sullen, morose, and heavy. He looked at me without words, clearly alarmed by what he was seeing on my countenance. I felt a depth of load that was too much for my body to bear. I turned away, silently, and went to the bed. As I started to lay my body down the water breached the dam. A massive cascade of flow surged forth from me. The colossal pool of accumulated dysfunctional living that had been my life seemed to flow from me all at once; fear of father, not being good enough, incapable, unable, isolated, gay, faggot, AIDS, Leslie the Faggot, hiding, lying, disease, incurable, recurring, RRP, loss of voice. In that instant, as my body cascaded onto the bed, it had all become too much. My defense mechanisms failed. I had reached the tipping point.

I fell onto the bed, curled up in a tight fetal position and began to cry – a violent, fierce, uncontrollable cry. A wail without sound emanated from my body as it convulsed;

my head pounded against the bed. I felt cramping in my face as it grimaced with pain.

My boyfriend, alarmed by what he was witnessing, lay down next to me on the bed and put his arm around me. He understood part of what was going on – everything associated with RRP – but did not, *could not,* understand the rest of it. As he experienced the complete and total breakdown that I was experiencing, he drew closer and held me tighter. I can remember completely releasing into his arms and feeling safe. It allowed everything in me to flow. I began to speak words to him, weak in their sound but comprehendible and powerful in their delivery. Words such as: tired, spent, don't know what to do, sad, afraid, done, helpless, lost. He comforted me as best as he could as the breakdown continued, in its entire enormity. I cried, wailed, thrashed and convulsed in that bed until I had nothing left.

It was a stripping away. It was a deconstruction of my thirty-year-old life. It was the dam breaking and the water violently cascading until nothing but the placidly flowing river remained. When the breakdown had run its course, I lay there, motionless and thoughtless. The sense of relief was extraordinary. I felt as if I had purged from the very base level of my existence. I was not aware of it at the time, but the lack of thought was a miraculous thing. I was simply too spent to think, too spent for my mind to embark on its conditioned path of continuous thinking. I eventually fell asleep.

## Defining Act

When I awoke my boyfriend asked me if I was okay and

then questioned me about what had happened in the bedroom. The conversation that ensued was deep and complex and had one defining outcome. It was time for me to come out to my parents. It was time to stop the hiding, lying, deceit and cover-ups. It was time to start living my life as the person that I was, and coming out to my parents was the defining act that needed to happen. For the first time in ten years, since I had come out to myself, when I thought about telling my parents, I was not immediately incapacitated by fear. I could feel, for the first time, a sense of relief and peace around the disclosure of my sexuality to the people who brought me into this world and raised me. One of the outcomes of the breakdown was clear; many levels of fear, many levels of my Complex, had been dismantled. That dismantling had allowed for a new light to shine. I began to formulate a coming out letter in my head.

It took me several days before I could put a pen to paper. In the interim, my friend who owned the Chris Craft and threw the *Opening Day of Boating Season* party on the boat called me. He told me that he had noticed the difficulties that I was having on the boat with regard to my inability to speak. "It was that obvious?" I said to myself while listening to him. He went on to tell me about a personal growth program that he had participated in and had reaped many benefits from. He suggested that I attend as a way to help myself deal more effectively with the realities of RRP and voice loss in my life. He was a good friend and I trusted him. I took his advice and enrolled in an upcoming program. It would be my first significant step into a long, rich and enduring path of recovery.

I had made the decision that the mode of reveal to my parents would be a letter. I could not do it over the phone as it was too impersonal. I could not do it in person as a face to face confrontation was too laden with fear. The letter would let me state what I wanted to say and then give them time to formulate a response. My mind thoughts revolved with words and sentences and a panoply of emotions ensued. What to say, how much to say, how to say it, tone, and delivery style. The more I thought the longer and more complex the letter became. The longer and more complex the letter became the more difficult the writing came to be. It reached a point where it was debilitating, and I could not produce an end result.

I remember the frustration leading me to a point where I told myself to stop thinking about what I was writing and just write. Keep it simple, I told myself, and that was the turning point. I wrote what appeared to me at first to be a ridiculously simple letter. Straightforward, factual, short, direct and to the point in its reveal that I was a homosexual man. The letter ended by asking them to call me when they were ready and able to talk. My judgment that the letter was ridiculously simple caused me to put the completed letter down, telling myself that I would return to it later after what I thought would be the benefit of additional time and thought.

Thinking about the letter was an exercise in frustration. My mind wanted to make it more complex, more literary, more substantial – more worthy. My thoughts told me that the letter had to be *very special*, and I struggled in my mind to make it so. Frustrated, I gave the letter to my boyfriend to read in order to get his feedback and opinion. To my surprise, he said it was clear and beautiful and that no changes or additions were needed.

I came to realize that the letter was finished and that it was ready to mail. I took it to the post office early the next morning and decided to send it via *next day* delivery. I had come to the point where I wanted them to know as soon as possible; waiting for a letter to go from one coast to the other via standard U.S. mail was more time than I could bear to endure.

I stood at the mail slot, poised to put the addressed and metered envelope into the hole. As my arm rose to the slot, the accumulated mental and emotional history of my life journey thus far rose up with it. I felt the dense energy of fear and dread well up in me. Soon, my parents would know that I am gay. How would they react to the news? What would they do? What would I *lose*? Thoughts in my mind charged forward with abundant frequency. Why was I taking such a risk? Why was I setting myself up for so much pain? Why was I inviting rejection and judgment? Would the pain of loss and retribution be even greater than the pain of hiding and deceit?

My hand trembled as I rested the lip of the envelope on the edge of the slot. I descended into a place of full blown Complex activation – my mind in overdrive, emotions raging and physical symptoms triggered – sour stomach, nausea, tight and labored breathing.

Then, a recollection. I remembered my breakdown on the bed and the momentary peace that I achieved after my complete mental and emotional deconstruction. I recalled the intensity of that peace. Standing there at the slot, nearly incapacitated by my raging Complex, I realized that I wanted more of that peace and that the letter was a doorway to it – *no matter what my parents' reaction ended up being*. I realized that the freedom from hiding and deceit that coming out would provide was more about me than them, more about my health and wellness than their potential judgments.

I pushed the letter into the slot. I heard *sllllliiit* and *thunk* as the letter slid through the slot and landed in the mail bin on the other side. I backed away slowly, staring at the mail slot while coming to a full realization of what I had just done. I was once again lost in my world of mind thought, completely unaware of my surroundings. As I took my next unconscious step backwards, I felt a sudden and startling presence under the heel of my left shoe. "Excuse me sir," rang out the voice of the woman standing behind me as she moved the toe of her shoe out from under the heel of mine. I had backed right into her. Jolted from my mind thought stupor, I realized what I had done to her, quickly apologized, turned on a dime and exited the post office with great haste.

## Another Person Who Could Not Speak

I knew I had to keep myself very busy for the next twenty-four hours, keeping my mind occupied as much as possible so it would not dwell on what was to come. From the post office to the location of my new job was a short walk, and I covered it in no time. I walked into my office and set about occupying myself with learning and performing the tasks of my new position. I had secured an entry level clerical support job with the Federal Government. The primary tasks of the job – filing, data entry, mail sorting – required very little speaking and thus the job was a good fit for me and my lack of voice. It was a humbling experience having gone from a position as Director of Sales and Marketing, making a substantial salary, to a position of clerical support, making a dollar above the minimum wage. But, it was a big relief to have a job that at least paid a little more than the meager disability payment that I had from my previous job. It also provided reasonable health insurance coverage, which had become a necessity in order for me to be able to deal with RRP. I was very grateful for the job.

After a day of work, I met my boyfriend and we filled the evening with dinner, talk and a movie. He knew and understood the profundity of mailing the letter, and he worked hard to help me fill the time. He spent the night at my apartment, as I did not want to be alone, and I endured a restless night's sleep as I tossed and turned continuously in the bed. My mind built scenarios around the possible responses that my parents would take and I could not find sleep until deep in the night.

I awoke in the morning, groggy from a short night of sleep, and hurried off to work. I filed, sorted, mailed and entered data with abandon during the day, trying to keep myself as occupied as possible. As the morning progressed into afternoon I could feel the dense cloud of *dread* start to balloon within me. Had it been twenty-four hours since I mailed the letter? – *Yes*. Is it possible that the letter has been delivered? – Y*es*. Could my parents have read it, or be reading it now as I think this? – *Yes*. Is it possible that right now, at this very moment, that my parents know that I am *gay*? – YES! How are they reacting? What are they doing? Are they angry? How hurt are they? Will they call and speak to me as I asked in the letter?

    I left work spun up like a top and wanted a drink very badly but thought better of it. I wanted a clear head in the event that they called me that evening. I headed home to my apartment and, soon after I arrived, my boyfriend appeared to keep me company for the evening. He knew how monumental this coming out was for me, how laden with anxiety and fear it was for me. He cooked me dinner and stayed at my side. We both waited with anticipation; waited for a phone call that we were not sure would come. I paced the room, watched TV, cleaned – anything to fill my mind and occupy the time. The evening progressed and my thoughts turned to the inevitable – surely by now they had the letter and they knew that their son, their only child, was gay. These thoughts terrified me. The surge of energy that welled up inside of me was composed of the sharp bite of worry, the deep throb of humiliation and the sting of rejection. If they had the letter, why had they not called? By this time it was late in the evening on the east coast. Were they too devastated to be able to respond? Were they formulating a response plan? What would it be? Would it be *no* response?

    My suffering mind and acute emotions must have translated to my body language. My boyfriend picked up on my distress and asked me to sit down with him on the couch.

"What can I do to help you calm down?" He said. I opened my mouth to respond and...

The phone rang. A blistering shock of piercing ringtone permeated the room and reverberated deep into my body. I looked at him and he looked at me. I felt a fire explode up into my head as my emotions ran roughshod. I became physically paralyzed by fear and unable to move from the couch to answer the phone.

The phone rang again, startling me into the realization that the time had come to answer the phone. The time had come to see who was on the other end; after all, it might *not* be my parents. But it might be.

"Are you going to answer that, you probably should," my boyfriend said to me, the strain of wary anticipation showing on his face. His question and statement was the impetus that broke me of my fear induced inertia. I got up from the couch; my body felt heavy and cumbersome, my movements labored. I moved to the phone, removed the handpiece slowly from the cradle and lifted it to my mouth and ear.

"Hello," I said in a weak, breathy voice.

"Craig this is Mum," said the voice of my mother. Her voice was trembling and unsure.

"Hi Mum," I said, barely able to croak out the words.

"We got your letter today. I need you to know that this is very difficult for us. It is going to take us some time to deal with this," she said in a sad and tremulous voice.

"I understand. Please take the time that you need," I said, with a hoarse and barely audible voice.

"I need to ask you something. Was there anything that we did wrong? Is there anything that we did to cause you to be *this way*?"

"No, I have been sexually attracted to men from a very early age, from my first memories of sexuality, actually," I replied. "You and dad did nothing wrong."

"I see," she said. She continued, her voice now muddled by tears, "Well, I just wanted to let you know that we got the letter and that we will need some time to deal with this right now."

"I understand. How is dad?" I said.

"He is having a difficult time. He can't talk to you right now; he just isn't able to do it."

"Okay," I said.

"I am going to let you go now," she said. "I love you."

"I love you too. Thank you for calling me."

Her voice cracked and trailed off as she replied, "Goodnight."

I slowly placed the phone back into the receiver and turned to look at my boyfriend. The look on his face was one of anticipation laced with trepidation. He raised his eyebrows and asked, "What did she say?" I stood there, motionless and unable to form words as my brain was completely engrossed in processing what had just happened. Enduring my lack of response, he waited for what for him must have seemed like an eternity. Finally he said, "Craig?" in an attempt to get me to respond.

"It's done," I said, the enormity of the words resonating deep inside me. The hiding, lying, denial and repression that had been going on for me with regard to my parents, since I was nine years old, was over. I felt a tremendous sense of relief. My boyfriend stood up, approached me and hugged me.

"Congratulations, that was a courageous, life-altering thing that you just did," he said as he held me in his embrace.

We released our embrace, and I slowly moved to the couch and sat down.

"She said she loved me," I said as I realized that one of my worst fears had *not* been realized – I had *not* been outwardly rejected by my mother.

"Wow, that is awesome," replied my boyfriend. "That is a really good sign. What about your father?"

His question hit me hard and shattered the sense of relief that I had been experiencing.

"She said that it was going to take some time for them to deal with this and that my father could not speak to me right now," I replied.

A startled look of concern came over my boyfriend's

face when he heard this about my father. *My* father – the guy who had an aggressive, gregarious personality that was larger than life. This outspoken, never at a loss for words man could not speak to me. Could not *speak*! I had never known my father to be incapable of speaking in *any* situation. It made me realize just how different this situation was and it terrified me. I then began to think about just how long it would take for them to *deal* with this situation, as my mother had put it. How long would my father be incapable of speaking to me? What would they think or do and what conclusions would they come to during this unspecified amount of time? My mind thoughts churned with images of my father and what he was doing and thinking and planning at this moment.

Then I became angry. "Fuck him," I remember thinking to myself. He wasn't there for me as a child so why should he be here for me now? Then I became embarrassed, then sad, then full of hurt that I had hurt them. Then the relief came back; a sense of accomplishment that I had finally come out to them. I felt a sense of freedom and healing. The range of emotions that were coursing through me was wide and far-reaching.

My boyfriend saw that I was lost in my churning thoughts and emotions. "I think the best thing that you can do is just give them the time that they need, however long that is," he said. His words resonated and pulled me out of my mind paralysis. I realized that he was right, the best and most appropriate thing to do was to let time pass and see where this all went for them.

"I am very proud of you. That is one of the most

difficult things you will ever do and you did it," he said to me. "Let's go outside for a walk so you can clear your head," he continued. That sounded like the best idea to me; how wonderful it would be to be able to *clear my head*. We walked out of the apartment and into the night. I felt like a door had opened and the potential for something positive and healing was at hand. Good thing, because with what was to come I would need as much positivity and healing as I could get my hands on.

# Big Wood River

## Responsibility and Accountability

A month had passed since my last appointment with my throat surgeon, and it was time for my checkup. My voice had improved some, but was still very raspy and weak. I sat in the surgeon's chair and prepared for the laryngeal scope. He inserted the instrument into me and put me through a series of vocal exercises while he examined my larynx, vocal cords and trachea. After what seemed like an interminably long exam he pulled the strobe out of me. He immediately handed me a tissue to wipe the pain induced tears from my eyes and said, "Well, I am sorry to say but another papilloma tumor has grown on your left vocal cord. That is why your voice quality has not improved much. We will need to do another surgery to remove that." My heart sank, fear swelled and disbelief ensued.

"Another tumor? Already? It has only been a month since my last surgery. How could it have grown so quickly?" I rasped, holding back more tears.

"Unfortunately this is what we can see with RRP. The tumors tend to reoccur, and sometimes they can reoccur quickly."

"Is there anything we can do other than surgery? Is there any kind of drug that might shrink or get rid of the tumors?"

"We do not know of any specific drug that will directly address the tumor growth. There is a series of drugs that we could try, but I need to have a frank discussion about them with you before you can make the choice of whether or not you wish to proceed down that road."

I became both frightened and hopeful. "Please tell me about the drugs," I said.

"They are chemotherapy drugs used in the treatment of cancer. They are used to arrest cancer cell production and cancer tumor growth. They might have an effect on the viral papilloma tumors, but our current evidence is inconclusive. We could try a round of one of these drugs, called Interferon, and see what happens, but you must understand that there are no guarantees."

The words chemotherapy and cancer rang in my head. Inconclusive evidence and no guarantees hung in my thoughts. I simply could not believe what was happening to me.

"You need to understand the side effects before you make your decision," he continued. "Interferon is a very powerful drug and the side effects will be nausea, body aches, joint pain and at times a feeling of all body illness."

"How long will the treatment last?"

"We will need to do a month-long trial, where the drug

will be administered several times a week. The drug is delivered through a shot in the abdomen. We will do the first one and then teach you how to give yourself the shot so that you can administer it to yourself."

I have no idea how wide open with astonishment my mouth was at this point in the conversation. I simply could not adequately process the road that was being laid out before me. All of this and no guarantee? No conclusive evidence that it would help? Shots in my abdomen?

"Do you think that you would like to try this?" he asked.

I thought about the fact that I had had two surgeries already and was now faced with a third, all in the span of two months. It was clear that the RRP was aggressive and tumors were growing frequently. My mind ended up clinging to the idea that chemotherapy at least presented a hope for tumor suppression, which had the potential to stop these surgeries and give me back some voice.

"You do believe that is has the possibility to help?" I asked.

"I believe that it is *possible*, yes," he replied.

"Okay then, let's try it."

"I will have my staff set you up with the Oncology department. I will work closely with the Oncologist, but they will be the ones that take you through the chemotherapy process, okay?"

I nodded my understanding.

"Again, I am sorry about all this. This is a difficult disease. We will do our best to help you with it."

As I said thank you to him, I could not contain my emotions any longer and tears came to my eyes. The enormity of what was happening and the road that I was about to embark on was too much for me to bear. The surgeon understood my trauma; I am sure he had seen it before. He placed his hand on mine, providing the comfort of his reassuring touch, and sat with me for a moment.

"We will take good care of you," he said.

Once I was able to compose myself, he led me to the desk of his assistant and instructed him to set me up with Oncology. The appointment would be the next day.

I spent the evening thinking. My mind created stream after stream of thought – never stopping and never subsiding. Worry, fear, questions, what-if scenarios, what would happen to me scenarios, future focused dramas – most of it tremendously damaging and dysfunctional, deepening my suffering. This process was so intense that at some point in the evening I found myself completely exhausted, both physically and mentally. I remember sitting on my couch alone, desensitized, unfeeling and thoughtless. It was during this time that a powerful realization came to me; the result of personal growth work I had been doing combined with my life circumstances. I realized, at a very dramatic moment for myself, that it was possible that *I* had caused my disease. The long buildup of dysfunction that I had experienced in my childhood, combined with years of hiding, lying, self-loathing and denying my gay existence, further combined with all the trauma associated with AIDS and the death of my friend, had culminated in an expression of ill health for me – RRP. I thought it no coincidence that the disease began to manifest itself at the point in my life, thirty years old, where all of these elements came together to reach a pinnacle of suffering. There had to be a release somewhere. All the negativity, maladjustment and distress had been building up within me and it had to express itself somehow. I had not been capable of purging it; rather, I hid it. If I was not capable of finding a way to release the pain and suffering, then the inherent wisdom and intelligence of my body would find a way, and that way was RRP. My body took away my greatest defense mechanism – my voice!

This realization was both terrifying and hopeful. Terrifying in that I had this disease. Hopeful in that if I had caused it, perhaps there was a way to be free of it. But how?

The Interferon injections did indeed produce the side effects of nausea, body aches, joint pain and at times a feeling of all body illness. I learned how to insert the syringe needle into my abdomen and deliver the drug myself at home. For a month I barely managed work and did nothing else, while feeling the ill effects of the drug. It was a miserable experience. And it did not work. At my checkup at the completion of the month-long trial, the papilloma tumor in my larynx had actually grown. My surgeon said we needed to discontinue the Interferon, as it clearly was not stopping the growth of the tumor and the level of drug in my system was becoming too toxic for my body.

He then suggested another chemotherapy drug called Cis-Retnoic Acid. This drug had also demonstrated an ability to shrink tumors but came at it from a different chemical angle than the Interferon. He then explained to me the side effects – headache, fever, dry skin, dry mucous membranes (mouth, nose), bone pain, nausea and vomiting, rash, mouth sores, itching, sweating, eyesight changes. He told me that I would need to take the drug in pill form for a month. At that point we would evaluate the size of the current tumor and see if the drug had any effect.

Despite the dizzying description of the side effects that I would experience, my brain somehow focused on the fact that I would no longer have to give myself shots in the abdomen in order to take this drug. Pills were infinitely easier for me, and this new drug provided more hope, so I agreed to take it.

It made the side effects of the Interferon seem like a walk in the park. I was incredibly sick. My skin turned *yellow*; I looked very ill. I missed work. I did not go out. My Complex was constantly activated by my mind which spun up dysfunctional thought after dysfunctional thought. For that month, I suffered tremendously, but I endured the drug, always keeping a glimmer of hope that it was shrinking the papilloma tumor.

The month ended and the evaluation scope of my larynx came. The surgeon shook his head as he removed the strobe from my head and neck. "I am sorry, but the tumor is still there and it has actually grown," he said. The tumor had grown. *Grown*! "It is clear that the chemotherapy drugs have no effect on the papilloma tumors so I think it best that we stop them," he continued. "I am sorry that it did not work, but I feel that it was worth the try," he stated in conclusion.

Through the veil of my shock I asked him if there was anything else that we could try. He replied that he was not aware of any other treatments for RRP, and that it was time to remove the tumor surgically. I left his office mired in a thick soup of thought and emotion.

I had my next surgery to remove the new tumor. Because this was my third surgery, a surgery *cycle* became evident. The succession of events took the following form: scheduling the surgery with the surgeon's office; scheduling and partaking in a pre-surgery physical with my doctor; scheduling and partaking in the pre-surgery appointment with the anesthesiologist; making arrangements with work to take off time for all these appointments and for the surgery itself along with the recovery; making the necessary arrangements at work to cover for the fact that I would not be able to speak for at least a week; stocking the house with soft foods that were easy to eat with a sore throat; no eating or drinking the night before surgery; stretching out the head and neck prior to surgery to prevent neck strain; IV insertion, the administering of Versed to dull my anxiety and prepare me for anesthesia; *The Surgery*; waking up to a raging sore throat; the *inability to speak;* feeling the dullness of pain medication; recovering voiceless and alone; returning to work and dealing with the extra stress created by my inability to speak; some voice recovery about a month after surgery.

This cycle I would experience many more times. The cycle gave me a significant amount of free time during the surgery recovery stages and I used that time to research RRP. I wanted to find a cure. I dove hard into the waters of medical research and as I did, I learned that what the surgeon had told me was indeed true – there was no known cure. Then I stumbled upon an RRP newsletter that explored alternative treatments. Non-western medical treatments like naturopathy and homeopathy. I decided to reinvigorate my exploration of these new medical worlds.

## The Gift

With western medicine providing no answers, the next journey of my life involved a major exploration of alternative medicines and cognitive therapies. Over the next many years, I investigated and took part in homeopathic, naturopathic, Chinese and Ayurvedic medicine and medical treatments. I participated in Reiki, Chiropractic and dietary supplement therapy. I explored and participated in faith healing and astrology. These were tremendous learning experiences for me; exploring these new worlds opened up new ways of thinking, new avenues to better health and a more global way for me to look at the world.

Concurrently, I embarked on an intense cognitive therapy exploration. I finally found a therapist who I clicked with and he helped me tremendously. He helped me to understanding the significance of my background, why it had affected me the way it did and how it manifested in my life at that current time. He turned me on to a method of cognitive therapy called psychodrama which I participated in for several years. Psychodrama involved recreating scenes from my past by acting them out in play-like form. The other members of the psychodrama group would act as the other members in the scene and we would recreate scenes from my past, as if on a stage in a theater. We recreated many scenes including significant interactions with my dad, bullying episodes and traumatic gay experiences. At the end of the psychodrama, the therapists would act as interpreters and give feedback. It was an incredible learning process for me. It was akin to being there at the time of the incident and being able to be both a participant and observer as my current self in my current adult life. It was a window to much insight, personal discovery and an understanding of my Complex, how it developed and how it manifested itself in my life.

Psychodrama also taught me about support; how to ask for it and get it. I learned that American society does not make it okay for males to ask for and receive support from others, particularly from other males. Men are supposed to be strong and independent and figure things out on their own. To ask for and receive support was a sign of weakness. This resonated strongly with me as it was exactly how I was raised. Psychodrama and the therapeutic process showed me that the exact opposite is what is actually true. To be able to ask for and receive support is a window to authentic, deep and intimate relationships with other humans. It breaks down barriers, lifts people up and creates strong connections that resonate deeply. I learned that to be able to ask for and receive support is a tremendous strength and never a weakness. It was an extremely valuable lesson to learn, and I would put it into practice often because I would need it during these years.

The RRP was relentless. By the time I was forty-three years old, I had had sixty-three surgeries to remove papilloma tumors from my larynx. It just kept coming and coming. Surgery cycle after surgery cycle – from the initial step of tumor diagnosis via the laryngeal scope, through surgery and recovery, to work and dealing with the extra stress created by my inability to speak. Sixty-three times!

I asked for and received support from my therapy group members, friends and family. I would ask for them to come to the surgery with me and be with me in the pre-op room while I was getting my IV and talking to the anesthesiologist and surgeon. I would have several people there with me during each surgery prep, and the gathering came to have a positive and productive social aspect that was appreciated by me, my supporters and the hospital staff as well. I ended up going into surgery with a much healthier attitude.

Then they would be there for me when I woke up, waiting with me in the surgery recovery room and giving me whatever I needed. They would get me home comfortably and settle me into my home recovery. All of this set the stage for them to follow up with me during the days and weeks after each surgery.

At first, I could feel my resistance to asking for and receiving all this help during the surgery cycles. But eventually a profound change took place. It was necessary for me to become vulnerable to accept this support, and that vulnerability in me seemed to open the door to the expression of vulnerability in my supporters. It opened the door to more open communications between us; walls came down and the relationships blossomed into greater levels of trust, affection and love.

Then I began to ask for and receive support in my work environment. RRP had been devastating to my career. I continued in my government job and tried to move up the ladder. More times than I can count, my career advancement would be challenged by RRP. The inability to speak would present constant communication challenges: the surgery cycles would be disruptive to accomplishing tasks and reaching goals and the side effects from the various drugs and the mental and emotional drain of the disease would be a hindrance to my productivity. Once I understood the benefits that I was receiving from asking for and accepting support from others during the surgery process, I began to employ this same technique in the work environment. I would ask to pair with a coworker when setting out to accomplish a task or reach a goal. I would accomplish the non-vocal aspects of the work; research, writing, graphics, logistics. My coworker would accomplish the vocal tasks; conducting meetings, making presentations, telephone work. I then asked for support from management by requesting that they procure assistive technology to help with my voice: hand held microphone and speaker devices to help project my voice; artificial larynx devices to use when I could not speak at all.

The result of asking for this support in the work

environment was profound. People just opened up! The collaborations were productive and inspiring to all involved. My career began to thrive and over the years I moved up through several positions, reaching a significant management position in the office.

During these years, the gift of having learned how to ask for and receive support got me through the trauma of RRP and enriched my life in many ways. I came to realize that it was RRP that had given me this gift. This realization was a major breakthrough for me. It was the catalyst that allowed me to see further and understand that RRP had given me *many* gifts; the gifts of *therapy* and *alternative medicine* and all the learning and understanding about myself and the world that they had brought to me.

From under the stress, strain, fatigue, hopelessness, fear and isolation that had been my primary experiences resulting from RRP, welled up a new sensation – the healing vibration of gratitude. I began to be grateful for all the positive things that RRP had brought to my life. It was the beginning of one of the most transformational elements of my life – my gratitude practice. I sought to be grateful not only for the dramatic learnings from RRP, but for all of the abundance of life that was around me – even the small stuff. Especially the small stuff. I worked to bring gratitude into my life regularly and routinely – to make practicing gratitude a habit.

## Sun Valley

Then the universe opened up. In the time since I had revealed my sexuality to them, my parents had worked to accept it, and they made strong efforts to build a positive and loving relationship with me in this new reality. They accepted and embraced my partner and made him feel like a member of the family. During this time, my father and I discovered that we both had an interest in fly fishing and we decided to plan a trip together. It would be the first time that we would spend time together, alone with each other, since I came out.

We decided to go to Sun Valley, Idaho and fish the waters in and around that idyllic mountain valley. During the time with my dad, I discovered that fly fishing was more than just an interest that we shared; it was a force that created a bond between us. My dad had more experience than I, and he taught me much about the sport. His teaching method was so very different than when I was a child. When I was young, my dad would teach with aggression, force and employ strong consequences for failure. To learn something from my dad was to know fear. Now, as he taught me fly fishing techniques in Sun Valley, his methods were much more relaxed and supportive. I am not sure what precipitated such a dramatic change; perhaps it was because I was now an adult, perhaps he had mellowed with age, perhaps he had decided to make a change. Whatever the reason, one thing was clear to me; he was really trying to have a good relationship with me. He was really making an effort to create a positive connection between us. I felt a strong desire to do the same; to rise to the challenge of creating a new relationship with my father.

I used many of the techniques that I had learned in therapy to help me rise to this challenge. I realized that my father really did love me, and that in my childhood, he acted in ways that he thought were best for me. His parenting techniques may have had serious flaws, but he did the best he could with what he knew about raising a child. He always had my best interests in his heart. Instead of dwelling on the hurt that I had experienced as a result of his parenting, I chose to focus on the gratitude that I felt for the positive things that he had brought to my world. In particular, gratitude for all of the positive, joyful things that I was experiencing with him *now*.

And boy, oh boy did the joy come! We set out to find a fly fishing hole that we had heard about, located about ten miles north of Sun Valley, on the Big Wood River. We drove off the highway and onto a rough and bumpy dirt road that lead down to the river. Getting out of the car and walking to the riverbank, we were both astonished by the beauty of the scene in front of us. The Big Wood River was flowing cold and clear; a classic freestone western mountain stream. It was the fall of the year, and the water flow was low – perfect for fly fishing. The river banks were full of large, flat, white granite boulders – ideal platforms for casting a fly to a feeding trout. Farther back from the banks, cottonwood and aspen trees blazed yellow and orange, cloaked in their brilliant fall color display. The mountains rose on all sides, towering above the river. The mountainsides displayed their own dramatic color display, with the deep green of evergreen trees standing next to and contrasting with the radiant yellows of the aspen trees. Above it all was the dazzling Idaho mountain sky; high, open, cloudless, windless and vividly blue. We remained at the riverbank for a moment, taking in the visual scene and listening to the only sound, which was the persistent thrum of the river as its waters glided over its rocky bed.

We geared up for fishing. My father showed me how to *mend* a fly fishing line in a flowing river. Mending was a technique that was used to marry the fly line with the movement of the current. This allowed the fly, located at the end of the fly line, to move naturally with the flow of the river, making it more enticing to a feeding trout. It was a difficult technique to master. I watched my father as he put the technique to use in the river. He was good at it. He would cast his line and the brilliant white fly, a Parachute Adams, would gently alight on the surface of the water. He would mend the fly line to match the current, and the line and fly would flow as one, gently, naturally, downstream.

Whammo! A big, fat rainbow trout came flying up out of the water and devoured his fly. I watched the tip of my dad's fly rod bend toward the river as it strained against the force of the hooked fish. Swish! The trout again launched itself out of the water and into the Idaho sky, shaking violently as it tried to dislodge the hook. Slap! The big body of the fish hit the water and it dove deep, pulling hard on my dad's bent rod. I watched him play it beautifully. He skillfully tired the fish enough to bring it to the riverbank and grab it with the net. I ran to him and peered into the net. The rainbow trout was stunning; big, strong, meaty, healthy. The color was dazzling. The silver in its scales and the bright red stripe down its side caught the sunlight and the fish shimmered. We are catch and release fly fishermen, so my father quickly removed the barbless hook from the trout's mouth, placed the fish back into the water, and we watched it swim away with a dart.

We were pumped. The catch filled us with the energy of excitement and we quickly returned to the task at hand – casting and presenting our Parachute Adams to feeding trout.

I practiced mend after mend, trying to marry the fly line, fly and current. One of the great things about fly fishing is that you really *know* when you get something right. When the cast, presentation of the fly and line mending all come together, you can just *feel* it. You have created something that has become one with the river. *You* have become one with the river. It finally happened for me! I cast into the flowing current, my fly alighted onto the surface of the water like a natural insect would, and I mended the line so that the speed of the fly moving down the river exactly matched the speed of the current. I knew it. For a second or two I watched with fascination, as my fly gently, naturally, moved with the river.

Whammo! Just as had happened with my dad, the rainbow trout exploded out of the water and consumed my fly. I felt a tremendous pull on the end of my rod. My dad saw the take and he yelled from his position downstream, "Keep the tip of your rod up. Let the rod work for you!" I did as he said and I felt the rod go to work. The fish pulled *hard* and bent the rod sharply; I could not believe how strong it was. The hooked fish was swimming downstream and, to relieve the tension on the line and prevent a break, I found myself walking downriver. Swish! The trout rocketed out of the water and jumped high into the air, allowing us a good look at it. It was a *very* big fish. Slap! It hit the water and dove deep, pulling very hard downstream. I continued to follow it to relieve tension on the line. By this time, I had walked far enough downstream to reach my father's position. He coached me through the play of the next many minutes as the fish repeated, time and time again, its cycle of jumping and diving. We walked down the river together. I was eventually able to get the fish close enough to the riverbank where my dad was able to net it. Its bulk filled the entire net; the trout was striking in size, color and beauty. We stood there for a moment, just looking at it. But only for a moment, as it was important to return this magical creature to its world. I removed the barbless hook and gently placed the trout back into the crystal clear river water. It responded to the return of its freedom with a powerful slash of its tail, and descended into the whirl of the current. My father and I looked at each other. He had a smile on his face that was as wide as the Idaho sky. He patted me on the back and congratulated me on catching such a beautiful trout.

It was a thrilling experience to play that trout. It was a transformative experience to play that trout with my dad. It was a turning point in our relationship. It was clear to me that my dad was looking for and had found a way to improve our relationship – fly fishing was the vehicle. I could see that he was trying and was invested. It was also clear to me that I had a role in this transformation; to accept and move on from the past, embrace the present and encourage the new connection. Continuing with my gratitude practice, I became thankful to my dad for his efforts and for his love.

## Mumps, Measles, and Rubella

The universe continued to support. I learned of a new treatment being offered for RRP by a surgeon in Denver, Colorado. It was a radical, experimental treatment that had not been through any official clinical trial and was not approved by the FDA. It had however, produced dramatic results in patients that had received the treatment. The surgeon would conduct a standard surgery to remove papilloma tumors from the larynx and vocal cords, but then would inject the Mumps, Measles, and Rubella (MMR) vaccine into the tumor sites and then systemically into the entire body. The patient population was limited, but the results for those who received the treatment were dramatic; greatly reduced occurrence of papilloma tumors and, in some cases, total remission of RRP.

The treatment required several injections of MMR over the course of a year's time. The side effects seemed minimal but were unknown. Long term effects of the treatment were unknown. None of it was covered by my insurance and that, combined with the costs associated with travelling on multiple occasions to Denver from Seattle for surgery and recovery, required massive sums of out-of-pocket money that I did not have.

The universe continued to provide. My boyfriend, who had become my life (domestic) partner of many years, researched and discovered that his work insurance would cover the Denver procedure. In addition, his insurance had a domestic partner clause which meant that I could sign up and get benefits. From a financial standpoint, the new treatment became a possibility. I decided to go to Denver.

I travelled to Denver four times during that year. During the first three trips, I had surgery to remove papilloma tumors and then got the injections of MMR. On the fourth trip there were no papilloma tumors present and I just received the injections. The fact that there were no papilloma tumors during that fourth trip was encouraging. I can remember not allowing myself to get too hopeful or excited however. After what were now sixty-seven surgical procedures over fourteen years, I had had my hopes of no recurrence dashed so many times that it was difficult for me to imagine a life without RRP.

I went into remission. The papilloma tumors did not grow. Months passed, years passed – no RRP! The gifts of support, gratitude, therapy and alternative medicine that had come into my life as a result of RRP continued to manifest and grow, enriching my life.

Life had become so much better, but still I was troubled. The events of life would still activate my Complex and deliver dysfunction and suffering to me. I wondered deeply about the fact that the difficulties of RRP had been removed, I had learned much from my journey and was a healthier person, still the mental and emotional dysfunction and suffering remained. This wondering was a catalyst to continue my therapy and gratitude practice – to use these two modalities to keep searching for an answer. A way out of the suffering.

# Awakening

## The Watcher

The Universe responded to my efforts – with a *bang*! I was continuing my journey of self exploration when I came across a teaching, in the form of a written sentence that stopped me cold. The sentence read, *You are not the thoughts in your head*. It was from a book written by Eckhart Tolle, called *The Power of Now*.

I looked at the sentence with awe and disbelief. Of course I am the thoughts in my head. That is what we humans do – think! The human brain and the thinking that it is capable of is what sets us apart from all other life forms on the planet. I *am* the thoughts in my head; I think continuously. So, what could this teaching possibly mean, I wondered.

The teaching went on to state that the *voice in my head is not who I am*. It described this voice as being the constant stream of thought that my mind created and that was continuously *talking* to me. This resonated very deeply with me as *my* mind was constantly talking to me via the continuous, non-stop production of thought. I came to realize how very powerful this voice was in my life. It controlled *everything*! It was a stunning realization for me.

And then came the most shocking question of all. If I am not the thoughts in my head and the voice in my head is not who I am, then *who am I?* Who the hell am I? How can I be anything other than me? The question resonated deeply, sparked curiosity and was the catalyst to research and study further.

The next learning came in the form of a simple technique which told me to become *The Watcher* of my thoughts. I started to observe the thoughts in my head by watching them. It was easy to do once I became aware that I was capable of watching my thoughts. This technique started slowly, but quickly grew as the awareness of my thoughts began to cause a separation from them – *and all the suffering that they were capable of producing.*

I learned that in addition to being able to watch my thoughts, I was also capable of watching the emotions that those thoughts produced. I became the Watcher of my emotions. A dramatic life shift occurred for me when I started to watch my thoughts and watch the corresponding emotions that those thoughts produced and the interplay between those thoughts and emotions. As I watched the churning ball of energy that is produced in me as my thoughts and emotions interplay, I was then able to watch – to *see* – the corresponding effects on my physical body. I was able to see the impulses to take physical action and to create specific behaviors that were produced in me.

As the Watcher, I became aware. The more I watched, the more aware I became. The more I watched, the greater the separation that occurred between me and my thoughts and emotions. It was a sense of *waking up*. Waking up to my thought patterns, to the emotions that they created and to the behaviors that would just automatically occur as a result of the interplay between the two. Instead of being dragged along like a wild river by my thoughts and emotions in this life, I began to see a way to the shore and out of the white water. Being the Watcher and waking up created a space between me and my constantly thinking mind. Being the Watcher created a gap between me and the mental/emotional Complex that had developed over the forty-five years of my life. It created a gap between me and *my* Complex.

The more I practiced being the Watcher, the easier it became to wake up to my thoughts and emotions as they were occurring in my daily life. I could catch my thoughts more quickly as they happened, watch the emotions that they created and feel the bodily impulses *as they arose* in my day-to-day living.

Then the third great learning of this period occurred. From Eckhart Tolle's books *The Power of Now* and *A New Earth*, I learned the key to staying out of my head; to stay out of the constant stream of thought that had been the experience of my mind for so long, and the resulting, never-ending flow of emotions and bodily actions that those thoughts would trigger. I learned of the primary key to reduce my suffering. That key was *the present moment.*

I came to understand that to be in the present moment was to be free of all the past and future mind thought that my mind was so good at producing. I realized that most of my thoughts had either a past or a future focus. Thoughts of the past would be triggered by my Complex. Thoughts of the future would be triggered by worry, anticipation, what-if scenarios. It was a remarkable discovery to learn just how much my thinking mind took me out of the present moment and into the past or future. To be in the present moment was to free myself from my mind. Instead of driving my car down the street engrossed in continuous thinking, I instead chose to focus on the present moment. I saw the trees, the blue sky, the cars around me, the colors, and the stripe of the road – really *saw* them. I heard the sound of the wheels on the pavement, the hum of the engine, the shifting of the gears – really *heard* them. I felt the rush of air on my face from the open window, I felt the firmness of the steering wheel in my hand, I felt the back of my thighs being supported by the edge of the seat – I really *felt* these things. I realized that when I focused on what was going on in the present moment, my mind activity greatly decreased, sometimes even stopped. Then the most remarkable transformation happened. I observed that I could actually *stop* myself from thinking. I could focus on the present moment and cease thought production. I realized that by being constantly lost in the dream of thought, that I was missing the richness and fullness of life that was all around me. When I focused on the present moment, the world around me became clearer, brighter, more alive, more abundant, and more rich. I also became aware of what an extraordinary relief it was to stop thinking!

Focusing on the present moment became my practice as I moved through the world in my day-to-day activities. Through the practice of present moment awareness I learned to use my mind as a tool and not let it use me. I began to use my human mind as the beautiful, wonderful thinking tool that it is, when I needed it, but then, shutting it off when thinking was not necessary. It was astounding to discover just how much I did not need to think during the course of any given day. It was doubly astounding to realize the amount of peace that was created in my life by reducing my thinking. It was remarkable to come to a full understanding of how my thinking mind caused me so much suffering, and how much that suffering decreased when I became *in* the present moment and thus stopped the thinking.

These new tools - realizing that I am not the voice in my head, becoming the Watcher, practicing present moment awareness and the cessation of thinking, transformed my life - and would be put to the test.

## Who Am I?

The MMR was a miracle. A year passed after the last treatment in Denver and no papilloma tumors grew. My speaking voice recovered – hoarse and weak from all the surgeries – but a speaking voice that could be counted on and thus once again used as a tool in life. It had been many, many years since I had been able to count on my voice being there for me. To have this tool returned to me opened up new doors in my career. I was able to participate in more social activities. It was all a tremendous breath of fresh air. A second year passed, and then the third with *no* papilloma tumors. I began to entertain the fact that I was cured. I continued the practice of incorporating the tools that I had learned; being the Watcher, present moment awareness, cessation of thinking, gratitude practice and giving and receiving support. The increased joy that occurred for me during this time was a catalyst for further personal and spiritual exploration.

And again, the Universe opened up. I was still exploring the question of, Who Am I? If I am not the thoughts in my head, the resulting emotions that the thoughts produce, and the mind-made self/ego that the interplay between the two creates, then who am I?

The answer for me came as I made further studies into the practice of being the Watcher. I continued to watch my thoughts and emotions and become conscious of them. My studies pointed me to some profound questions; when you are being the Watcher of your thoughts, who is the one who sees? Who or what is doing the seeing that is independent and outside of your thinking mind? Who or what makes you conscious of your thoughts and emotions?

These were deep-seated questions for me. I learned that the word *conscious* was the pointer to the answer. I noticed that when I became the Watcher, I accessed a place that felt very different from my normal state of living. This place felt mindless, thoughtless, open and free. It felt objective. In this place, I learned that I saw and interpreted the world through a *filter*. My *own* filter had been built over all the years of my life and had been formed by all my experiences in this world. I have heard this filter called many things – the Ego, the Self, the Complex. In this place, I could see the filter and realize that I could be separate and free from my Ego/Self/Complex – free from my filter. I came to understand that this place was a place of awareness. A calm, peaceful place of unlimited space and depth. A place that allows for *the knowing*, not what is *known*. A place that is about *being*, not thinking or emoting or doing. This place was *consciousness* itself - the One Force that I had experienced from the cold of the gold metal trigger. I learned that it was my conscious, indwelling *being* that was doing the observing. *Being* was separate and distinct from my physical form – a very different place from my physical form existence. I have heard *Being* called by other names; God, Spirit, Soul, the Universe. I think that these words are all pointers to the same thing, which I choose to call *consciousness*. It is the indwelling being force that allows me to be the Watcher. It is what allows me to *be*. It allows me to become *conscious of being conscious*. When I become the Watcher, I am seated in this place of consciousness!

As I continued to experience and put to the test this place of being the Watcher – this place of consciousness – learning and insight came to me like never before. I discovered a very deep well of peace that exists in the realm where the Watcher exists. A place of no fear, no anxiety, no suffering. When my Complex got activated, which of course it still did, I would now watch it. I would catch the thoughts as they arose and watch them. I would watch the corresponding emotions bubble up. I would watch the physical symptoms appear in my body. I would watch the suffering. I would watch this all from the place of the Watcher – from the place of consciousness. Then a very profound step occurred in my journey. As I watched from this place of consciousness, I began to see a space open up between my *being* and my Complex. I began to see that my Complex, this swirling ball of thoughts, emotions and energy that had formed over years of traumatic experiences in my life – *was not me*. The space that had opened up between me and the Complex allowed me to see the Complex and remain separate from it, as opposed to *not* seeing it and being drawn into it. This space, this awareness, this consciousness allowed me to see that I could make new and different choices with regard to my Complex. I could choose not to become involved with it. I could choose not to be drawn into the dysfunctional mental, emotional and bodily reactions that the Complex had caused, over and over again, so many times in the past. The space opened up the possibility for making a different choice.

And I embarked on making that different choice. I was amazed how easy it became *to* begin making that different choice. I came to understand that just by watching my Complex, just by being conscious of it and seeing the space between my true being and it, the strength and pull of the Complex diminished significantly. I began to realize that it was not *my* Complex, as I had so often thought, but that it was just *a* Complex that had *nothing to do with me*. Nothing to do with the conscious being that is truly *who I am*. It was a Complex that had been built by an unconscious thinking mind that had responded to environmental circumstances.

I made that different choice. And that choice was to come back to the present moment. The lesson of present moment awareness was the key to moving away from the dysfunction of the Complex. From the place of being the Watcher, I made the choice to focus my attention on the present moment. No past thought, no future thought, just immersion in what *is* right now. It was the most transformational moment of my life.

## A Test

I woke up one morning and said, "Hello," to my partner. No voice came out – just a whispered, "Hello." I felt a lump in my throat. I continued speaking to him, and the word sounds that came out were much more hoarse and weak than they had been the day before. I felt the familiar fullness in my throat that had accompanied the growth of papilloma tumors in the past. It had been three and a half years since my last MMR treatment. Three and a half years of better voice quality, no tumors, no surgeries, no RRP. During that time I had slowly, gradually come to believe I was cured of the disease.

As the day pressed on and my vocal quality did not improve I knew what was happening – all the signs were there, and it was undeniable. My mind went into hyperdrive thought production; the disease is back, the MMR is not a cure, I am not cured, another surgery cycle is coming, my job is more vocally intensive now so how will I do it. My emotions immediately followed; shock, sadness, anger, disappointment, fear, anxiety. The Complex became activated and my suffering began.

But this time it was different. I caught the thought production early on and became the Watcher of the thoughts and emotions. I watched the Complex and saw its churning ball of energy rise up inside me. I took the time to watch all this, look at it and say resolutely – *That is not me!* I don't have to buy into this suffering. I can squelch it now by coming back to the present moment. Instead of becoming lost in my head, I practiced full present moment awareness. I became aware of all that was around me. I engaged all five senses to *be here now*. I then chose to use my mind as the beautiful tool that it is and determine, from this place of present moment awareness, just what it was that I needed to do to take care of this current situation. No past thought, no future thought, just what do I need to do *now*. And what I needed to do was just so easy. I called my surgeon's office and made an appointment for a throat exam. That was all I needed to do. No drama and trauma as my mind would have provided if I had let it churn out its thoughts as I had done so many time before.

And I practiced this technique all the way through the surgery cycle that came. Instead of being mired in the suffering that could have been caused by the return of RRP, I remained the ever vigilant Watcher, stayed present, and stayed conscious. I was able to do a miraculous thing. I found a surgeon in Seattle that was willing to take on the still investigatory and non-FDA approved MMR treatment for RRP. I was able to convince her that the MMR had put me into remission for three and a half years and she agreed to administer the drug to me. Same protocol – three or four surgeries accompanied by three or four injections of MMR over the course of a year. I no longer had to go to Denver for the MMR! It was a tremendous improvement in my treatment plan, and I practiced gratitude for the opportunity.

Practicing that gratitude and the consciousness techniques that I had learned with regard to the return of RRP provided me with a tremendous new insight. As I exited my new surgeon's office in Seattle after having set up the next surgery, I realized once again that RRP was a gift. It was a gift that had taught me to *wake up*, to be *present* – to become *conscious*. It was a stunning revelation and it stopped me in my tracks. I navigated to the closest chair that I could find and threw myself down into it. I wept – tears of *joy*. Not tears of anxiety and suffering that for so many times had been associated with the surgeon's office, but tears of *joy*. Tears of *joy* in that RRP had shown me a way to be free of my human suffering. Not just free of the suffering that I had for so long endured from RRP, but a way to be free from any and all suffering in my life!

This insight was tremendous motivation to continue my spiritual studies. I began to study meditation and, as I did, I realized its many benefits. I found that meditation quiets the mind and allows access to consciousness. I also discovered that, for myself, I did not need to have a prolonged meditation session in order to reap these benefits. I found a short, four and a half minute guided meditation that I used first thing in the morning as a primer to bring the present moment, the Watcher and conscious awareness into my upcoming daily activities. The key was to bring the present moment, the Watcher and consciousness into my daily living, not just while sitting in a quiet room somewhere during my meditation. The meditation also helped with the cessation of thinking during my day-to-day activities. I learned to create as many *mind gaps* in my stream of thinking as I could during the course of the day. I learned to spend as much time during the day as possible with *no mind*. This short meditation was a primer to help with that.

And boy, oh boy, would I put all this to the test. Over

the next year I had three surgeries to remove papilloma tumors and receive MMR injections. It was a transformational time for me as the second of the two surgeries had been severe in that the number and size of the tumors was dramatic. It pushed my vocal cords over the edge. This seventy-fifth surgery had reduced my vocal capacity and capabilities to a new low.

During the three and a half years that I had been in remission, I had taken a new Federal job that was much more vocally intensive than previous positions. It was now clear that I could no longer do the job, and my surgeon told me so. In fact, my surgeon told me that I should no longer do any job that required me to use my voice on a regular basis, or to rely on my voice as a tool in life. It became evident that what I needed to do was retire from my job. After nineteen years of working for the U.S. Government, I made the decision to put my health first, and I retired from Federal service. It was a very difficult decision to make. As had happened so many times in the past, this newest challenge was the catalyst to continue with my self-help and spiritual studies. And, as had happened so many times in the past, when I made the effort, the Universe opened up.

I learned about three ways of wise living. Three ways of living that fit beautifully into my consciousness practice. The practices of Acceptance, Non-Resistance and Non-Judgment.

I learned the power of accepting what *is* and what life brings. The power lay in not resisting and not judging what *is* and what life brings my way. I applied it to my act of retiring from work. I accepted that retirement was the next step in my path, and I did not resist it. I did not judge myself or resist the process of retiring. I accepted that the RRP had returned, had damaged my vocal cords and impacted my ability to speak. I didn't resist it or fight it. I did not judge myself for any of it.

What an incredibly liberating action this turned out to be. I realized that I had spent so much of my life resisting, judging and not accepting that which happened to me. I had put so much time and energy into opposing what life brought my way.

I realized the incredible power that comes forth by deciding to take action and move forward in life from a place of acceptance, non-resistance and non-judgment. It was a completely different experience from trying to take action and move forward when so much of my energy was being used for the opposite. I discovered that it takes an incredible amount of energy to resist life. By not resisting, all that energy became available to me!

When it came time for the fourth of the four surgeries in this MMR treatment protocol, I went to my surgeon's office for my pre-surgery exam. I sat in the exam chair and the surgeon sent the laryngeal scope down into my larynx. The news was good in that I had only one small tumor on my left vocal cord. And then the next journey, the next test of all my *consciousness* learning began.

My surgeon said to me, "I would like to talk to you about a new procedure that we might use to treat that tumor as opposed to the normal surgery that you have always had."

"Something new?" I said to her. It was so infrequent that there was anything new with regard to the treatment of RRP that I was surprised and my interest was piqued.

"Because the tumor is so small, I would like to try and treat it with the MMR right here in the chair. I do not think that I need to surgically remove it, but I would like to inject it with the MMR."

"No surgery," I replied. "Bring it on. How do you treat it here in the chair?"

She paused and breathed deeply. "Well, what I propose is that I insert the laryngeal camera scope into your larynx so that I can get a clear picture of it. I will hook up the scope to this computer and I will be able to see the images of your vocal cord and the tumor, *live*, right here on this computer monitor (she pointed to the CPU and monitor that was next to the exam chair)."

"Great, that sounds pretty normal. I have had over one hundred laryngeal scopes in my life so, believe it or not, I am used to them by now."

"Then comes that second part of the procedure. I will insert a needle into your throat, guide it to the tumor using the camera images on the screen, and inject the MMR into the tumor."

My breath caught and my heart skipped a beat. She was proposing to put a needle into my throat – all the way into my larynx!

"Will I be awake during this procedure?"

"Yes, you need to be awake so that I can work with you while I am guiding the needle and injecting the tumor."

I shuddered.

"Can we do this right here, right now?"

"Yes, right here in the chair."

"And this will prevent me from having a surgery?"

"If the MMR keeps working like it has, my hope is that it will shrink the tumor and we will be able to avoid surgery – yes."

My mind began to spin with thought. I began to comprehend all the benefits of *not* going through a surgery cycle. I began to think of all the pain and discomfort associated with the course of action that she was proposing. And then I caught myself. I became the Watcher. I watched my thoughts and all the emotions that were coming up. I watched the ball of mind and emotional energy that had been created within me in just the last minute or two. I decided not to participate in the drama and brought myself back to the present moment. I decided that I had an opportunity in front of me. Not just an opportunity for a new treatment method, but an opportunity to use all that I had learned while undergoing the procedure.

"Okay," I said. "Let's do it."

"Great. Don't worry; we will take very good care of you."

She called her assistant into the room. While the

assistant was preparing the room for the procedure, the surgeon stepped out. She quickly returned with a syringe in her hand – it was a *large* syringe. The cap on the end of the syringe was long, indicating the length of the needle that it was protecting. My reaction was swift and penetrating. My mind said, "Shit, that's a big needle." Fear and anxiety quickly welled up in me. I watched it all. I saw my separateness from the mind thought and emotions and realized *that they were not me*. I returned to the present moment. I focused on staying in the present moment. No future thought of what I *thought* was to come. Just present moment awareness of what was going on and happening in the room as the activity unfolded. Focusing on the present moment allowed me to stop thinking. I just did not think and oh, what a relief it was. To be out of my head, out of my mind, free of my thoughts. Just *being*, as I sat there in the chair watching, hearing, feeling, smelling, experiencing – but not thinking!

It was time for the laryngeal scope to be inserted into my larynx. The surgeon skillfully guided the tip into my nose and navigated it through my sinus cavities and down the back of my throat into my larynx. I was positioned so that I could see the images on the computer monitor. The camera was working beautifully. You could readily see both my vocal cords. There was not much left of them, the result of damage from the papilloma tumors as well as what now had been seventy-six surgeries to remove them. I could also see, quite clearly, the tumor that was hanging from the left cord.

The surgeon then passed the handle of the scope to her

assistant and directed her to hold it still and in place. She picked up the syringe and removed the protective cap from the needle. It was a very long needle. I focused intently on the present moment. I did not allow my mind to produce thoughts. She then turned to me in the chair.

"Okay, we're ready. I would like you to remain as still as you possibly can. Do you think you can do that?"

"Yes," I replied. I was astounded at how calm I was. The lack of thought, the resulting lack of emotions and resulting lack of bodily reactions was creating a *very different experience* than if my mind had been in control. A much more peaceful experience. Then it dawned on me. I will meditate while this is going on. I will actually go to my place of *being*, not thinking or emoting or reacting. I will go to the place where my Watcher resides. I will go and seat myself in consciousness by just *watching* the physical feelings and experiences that come up as this procedure is performed on my body. If my mind produces thoughts and emotions and my body creates reactions, I will just watch them and not become involved with them. I will stay seated in present moment watching consciousness.

She raised the needle to my throat and inserted it in the vicinity of my Adam's Apple. I felt a prick, then a sting. I focused intently on the present moment and stayed in the place of my Watcher. I felt a strange discomfort as the needle penetrated the walls of my throat and my larynx. I watched the discomfort, dismissing any thoughts that arose.

"Okay I am in your larynx now," she said. "I am going to move the needle so that I can get a clear shot at the tumor. Stay with me, you are doing great." She watched the computer monitor, seeing the needle inside my larynx. She guided the needle toward the tumor.

I felt strange, unfamiliar sensations within my throat. I just watched them. I watched the energy of these sensations. I did not think about them. I stayed completely present to what was going on. My mind did not engage with thought. And then, I felt pain. An honest to goodness shot of real physical pain.

I watched it. It was a miraculous experience for me to watch pain with present moment awareness. I came to realize, in an instant, that pain is just another form of energy in the universe. And that is *all it is*, just another form of energy. It does not have any more significance than any other form of energy in the universe. It was the thoughts that my mind produced with regard to my pain that made pain so powerful for me in the past. I continued to watch the pain energy, just be present with it and not think about it. As I did this I witnessed a space open up between me in my true place of being, and the pain. I realized that the *pain is not me. No* pain is me. It comes and it goes just like any other form of energy. It has nothing to do with *who I am!* It was a miraculous revelation for me, sitting there in that exam chair with a needle stuck in my throat.

"Got it," she said as she successfully injected the MMR into the papilloma tumor.

I felt a momentary sting as she withdrew the needle from my throat. She pulled the syringe away from my neck and placed it on a tray. It was over and done, just like that.

"You did great. You stayed very still and I was able to get a clear shot and inject the tumor with MMR – nice job," she exclaimed. "Now you can just come back in a month and we will see what the results are."

I expressed my gratitude to her. I told her what an amazing surgeon she was, how wonderful the staff was and how grateful I was to have had the experience and the opportunity for this new treatment. She only knew the half of my source of gratitude!

I left her office feeling a deep sense of peace. The experience had been transforming for me. RRP had given me another profound gift.

And the gifts continued.

## Compassion

My partner's father had rejected and disowned him at an early age because my partner was gay. His father was a fundamentalist Christian and used his faith as a basis for justifying the rejection and disowning. In the twenty years that my partner and I had been together, he had never acknowledged my presence in any way. I had never met him. The only interaction from him would be an occasional letter, directed to my partner, asking him to enter the gay-to-straight conversion program offered by his father's church. I can remember feeling great anger and fear towards him over the years. He represented all the bullying and homophobia that I had been exposed to as a child and adult. He activated the Complex. I had come to learn from my partner and other members of my partner's family that the father had experienced a difficult childhood, and that he carried the wounds from his childhood into his adult life. He had experienced failed marriages and strained relationships with his children. I came to realize that, *just like me*, he had a significant Complex/Ego/Self that had a profound effect on the actions that he took in life. His Complex/Ego/Self was powerful and dysfunctional just like mine; it just manifested itself in different ways than mine. And then I came to understand that, just like me, his Complex/Ego/Self *is not him*. He is the same *being* that I am. He just has not had the opportunity to wake up, to become the Watcher, to become aware of his Ego/Self/Complex. He has not yet become conscious. It dramatically changed the way I felt about him. I no longer felt anger and fear towards him, but rather, compassion. Compassion for all the suffering that he endured in his life as a result of him being unaware of his Complex/Ego/Self.

This was a profound realization for me because I came to understand that this was the case for many people on this planet. Many people, I think, have their own Complex/Ego/Self that is at work in their lives and they are not aware of it, or, do not know how to become free of it. This realization has changed how I feel about and interact with all people. Especially when I see people take damaging, hurtful or dysfunctional actions. Instead of responding to those actions with anger, fear or some other negative reaction - the Complex within me being activated, I instead try to respond with compassion, realizing that *that is not them!* It is their Complex/Ego/Self that is causing them to take the damaging, hurtful or dysfunctional action. It is not really who they are. I may not agree with the action, but I don't get activated by it. I try not to *react* and go to the negative place that my own Complex/Ego/Self would have taken me to in the past. Instead, I am conscious of what is going on, I feel compassion for the person's suffering, and then I move forward from that place. This has changed how I interact with people. I can remember creating intensely negative thoughts and emotions about people who had wronged me, hurt me in some way, or took actions or positions that I did not believe in or agree with. Anger, frustration, fear, anxiety and worry would all come up for me, and I would take action from that place of strong negative dysfunctional energy. More often than not, the creation of more anger, frustration, fear, anxiety and worry would be the result. *Compassion* from an understanding that the action does not come from the *being* that this person truly is, creates an entirely different energy that can be used to move forward. It creates a positive, non-reactionary energy that I have found has the ability to transform negative and difficult personal interactions. It is energy that does not ignite, it unites.

## Really Seeing Him

My partner and I had been together for twenty years and we decided that we wanted to mark the milestone with a celebration. We wanted an event that was unique and meaningful. We had never been able to get married as same sex marriage had not been allowed in Washington State. We decided to have an event that was a combination of a *Commitment Ceremony* and an anniversary party.

Several years before, we had purchased a piece of land

in the Cascade Mountains and we decided to have the ceremony and party there. The land was located in a mountain vale called Hidden Valley. It truly was hidden. You could only access the valley via a small and rough dirt road. The valley is comprised of a flat, green grass filled meadow with a cold and clear mountain stream, Swauk Creek, running through it. The creek is lined with mature aspen and cottonwood trees and is a haven for wildlife; trout and salmon ply the water and deer, cougar, elk, turkeys, and bear inhabit the riparian area. At the edges of the valley the Cascade Mountains slope upwards, isolating the valley and reaching toward the deep blue, clear sky. The rising slopes are covered with ponderosa pine trees, the deep red hue of their bark contrasting sharply against their dark forest green needles. There are no structures or development in the valley as the land has been preserved in a conservation trust.

We had spent many years enjoying this land by camping, hiking and exploring the valley. It had become a very special place for us, and we deemed it the perfect place to hold our ceremony.

The planning and execution of our event brought a new opportunity for my partner and me, the opportunity to bring the understandings and teachings that I have discussed in this book, to the planning and execution process of our event. Even more than that, to bring those understandings and teachings to a greater depth in our relationship. My partner and I had been sharing our consciousness journey over the preceding several years, and this event proved fertile ground for applying all the techniques that we had learned.

The event turned out to be a powerful source of emotion and thought for me. It was a commitment ceremony (a wedding if it could have been), an anniversary party, and a life celebration – all rolled into one event. It was a big deal.

During the planning process with my partner, we had many discussions about the details of the event. Frequently during these conversations, I would have moments where my mind would start to fill with thoughts, emotions would be triggered and at times, the Complex would be activated. At those moments, I learned of a new power that the present moment can give to an intimate relationship. The power to be with someone totally. By being the Watcher and distancing myself from my thoughts and emotions, I could be with him in these conversations in a complete way. Instead of thoughts swirling through my head and thinking about what I was going to say next as he spoke, I had a quiet mind as he spoke. I was there with him totally. I could really *see* him as he spoke; really listen to what he was saying. I could watch his body language, hear the sound of his voice and be completely present in the room with him. The key to all of it, was having no mind thought. I could see him clearly without looking through the filter of my thoughts and emotions. It was an incredibly intimate experience. I experienced my being connecting with his being. I experienced a consciousness connection with him. I found that when he had finished speaking, I could allow my thoughts to return and the response that I formulated and spoke was clear and peaceful. The conversation would continue in this manner and it gave me the opportunity to employ acceptance, non-resistance and non-judgment to his words and actions during the conversation. Using those techniques in combination with being completely present with him while he was speaking transformed the conversation. My removal of mind thought, judgment, non-acceptance and resistance from the conversation, and then moving forward from that place, fostered a depth of peace and connection in my exchange with him that I had not experienced before. It was exhilarating and liberating. It was incredibly intimate.

I have endeavored to bring these techniques to all areas of our relationship since, as has he, and the result has been profound. Connection, intimacy, peace and love within the relationship have all been magnified.

## The Way Out

It had been about nine months since I had received my last MMR injection, which had been by the needle inserted into my throat. My vocal quality was as good as could be expected, and I had no reason to believe that any tumors were growing. Based on the vocal quality evidence, it appeared that the MMR was working once again. It was time for a checkup, and I went to my surgeon's office. She inserted the laryngeal scope into my nose, and put me through the standard round of vocal exercises while she examined my larynx. She removed the strobe and said, "Well, you have three papilloma tumors in your larynx." She had recorded the images from the scope camera and pulled them up on the computer monitor. She described the location of the tumors to me.

"You have one tumor here (she pointed at the screen)

just below your right vocal cord. The other two tumors are down here (she pointed) on the wall of your larynx. None of these are on your vocal cords, so they are not impacting your vocal quality. They are not yet big enough to impact your airway and your ability to breathe, so I would like to just let them be at the moment. I do not think we should do surgery right now. Let's monitor them and see what they do. If you have any new symptoms before your next appointment with me, such as additional voice loss or difficulty breathing, come back and see me right away, and we will get you into surgery."

In the past, this type of diagnosis from the surgeon would have produced tremendous mind thought production within me. It would have produced deep levels of fear, anxiety, worry and depression in me. It would have activated my Complex/Ego/Self. I would end up suffering tremendously as my mind and emotions swirled out of control as a result of this *bad* news. This news in particular, was charged more than most as it delivered the message that the MMR was no longer working as well as it had in the past, or quite possibly was no longer working at all.

My mind and emotions started to go to these old familiar places as I sat in the exam chair and absorbed this news. But this time was different. This time I caught the mind thought and upwelling emotions early, right as I was sitting in that chair. I became the Watcher and I observed the thoughts and emotions. I became conscious of them. I saw them for what they were, just another form of energy in the universe. I saw the space between me, my *being*, and this thought and emotional energy. I then realized that this energy was not me, and I did not have to buy into the drama of the thoughts and emotions. I did not have to participate in the fear, anxiety, worry and depression. I made the conscious choice, sitting there in the chair, not to buy into it. I then made another conscious choice and chose to come to the present moment. To immerse myself in the *is*ness of this moment. To be here – totally. I made the choice to accept this present moment without judgment or resistance. The present moment proved to once again be the key, the avenue, to stay clear of the Complex/Ego/Self. *The suffering stopped.* I engaged with my surgeon and her staff completely, doing what I needed to do to set up my next appointment. I walked out of her office and into the outside air experiencing all that there was to experience with my five senses. When my mind would produce worrisome thoughts about the future, I dismissed them. When it produced anxiety producing thoughts about the past, I dismissed those as well. I just did not buy into my mind thoughts and continuously brought myself back to the present. I stood there on the sidewalk, looking at the beautiful bright blue sky, feeling the cool Seattle wind on my face and realized for the first time, after twenty years and seventy-six surgeries, that I was free from RRP. It would no longer exercise the control and influence over me, through the power of my unconscious thinking mind, that it had in the past. Whether or not the disease would continue to physically manifest itself in me became irrelevant at that moment. I was free of it no matter what. And it was bigger than that. I realized, standing there on that beautiful Seattle sidewalk, that I now had the tools and the ability *to be free of any and all suffering* in my life. *Consciousness* was the way out of suffering.

I came to realize through this exercise of coming to the present moment, that the present moment *is all I really have*. Anything else, past or future, is just a product of my thinking mind and the Complex/Ego/Self that it built. I learned that a tremendously liberating experience was to practice the following; wherever I am, be there totally; whatever I am doing, use all of my senses to be in that moment.

Becoming aware, waking up, becoming conscious and practicing present moment living continued to be a catalyst for my studies. Through Michael A. Singer's book, *The Untethered Soul*, I learned that not only did I have the choice *not* to buy into the dysfunctional drama of the Complex/Ego/Self by coming to the present moment, but at the instant when I came to the present moment I had the opportunity to make another choice. I could make the choice to be *open*. I could choose to remain open to what I experience in the present moment. I could make the choice not to judge or resist or not accept what I discovered in that moment, and then, remain open to that discovery. Being open is the opposite of being closed. Being closed is resisting, judging and not accepting the *is*ness of the present moment. It is tightening up and fighting against what is. Being open is to accept willingly and freely what the present moment brings. It is greeting it with willing and open arms, and then moving forward from that place of openness. I discovered that to move forward from this place requires much less energy than to try to move forward from a place of being closed. In fact, being open to the present moment *provides* energy for movement and action. I realized that the act of resistance, judgment, and non-acceptance of the present moment – the place of being closed – is an energy suck. It takes a tremendous amount of energy to resist life. Openness does just the opposite; it *provides* energy for taking action in life.

Through this practice I came to understand just how closed I had been to life over the course of my life thus far. I understood just how much energy I had put into resisting, judging and not accepting the events and manifestations of my life: childhood bullying, homosexuality, RRP. To stop doing this has been a tremendously liberating experience. To stay open to life instead of being closed to it has dramatically reduced the activation of the Complex/Ego/Self. It has allowed for more positivity and less negativity; more happiness and joy.

And speaking of happiness – I have found this to be another powerful choice. I discovered through reading *The Untethered Soul*, that the choice to be happy is a choice that I can make every day and in every situation.

## The Canyon

I recently travelled to the Grand Canyon to do a backpacking trip. I hiked down into the Canyon all the way to the Colorado River, spent three days walking along the river and exploring slot canyons, and then hiked back up to the Rim. I did this trip with the people that became my friends during my college years at the University of Vermont. We get together every five years and go on a backpacking trip. We leave our spouses and children at home and immerse ourselves in exotic places like the Canadian Rockies or Alaska. We spend very high quality time together and have deep discussions about our journey through this life. These are the people that I described earlier; the people that I met in college and developed beautiful friendships with. The same people that I experienced fears and anxiety with, regarding the team sports of football, broomball, softball and hockey.

On one particular day in the Canyon, we were backpacking from our camp at the Colorado River to our next camp deep within a side canyon. The day was hot and as the day progressed toward noon time the blazing sun became scorching. We were within the inner gorge of the Canyon, hiking on a bench several hundred feet above a small ravine, fully exposed to the sun. There was no wind. The Grand Canyon magnifies sun and heat, and the environment was becoming stifling. Adding to the intensity, the trail suddenly increased dramatically in grade and we were working hard to climb the trail in the relentless, suffocating heat. I discovered that, in my discomfort, my mind began to wander into negative thoughts; "Why the hell are we doing this trip at such a hot time of year? I don't think I have enough water; What if I overheat and get sunstroke? I am so uncomfortable; Where is that camp? We should be there by now; How much longer is it? Will the camp have shade? What if there is no water?" I began to resist the smothering environmental conditions, as if there was something that I could actually do about them. I felt my body tightening up and my breathing becoming more laborious. I was closing, both physically and mentally/emotionally.

Then I caught myself and became the Watcher. I saw the thoughts and realized that they were not me. I made the choice to stop resisting my current environment and state of physical body. I chose to accept the current situation and not judge it. I made the choice to come back to the present moment and open myself up to it. And at that moment, the Canyon became alive. I saw the beauty of the landscape I was travelling through. I felt the awesome power of geologic time that was on display in the plethora of rocks and Canyon formations that were all around me. By removing myself from the thoughts in my head, I was able to tap into the magnificence of the creation that was all around me and that I was a part of. I then took it a step further and decided to make the choice to be happy about the sun and the heat. I felt happiness flood my body as I became one with the present moment, which included the intense sun and high temperature.

Making the choice to be happy, I have come to believe, is a very powerful spiritual path. To be happy is to be open. If a situation in life arises that makes me angry, tense, worried, frustrated or activates the Complex, such as what I was experiencing in the heat of the Grand Canyon, I practice gratitude for the opportunities that these situations and energies provide. *The opportunities to wake up and become conscious.* And *that* is something to be very happy about. For me, bringing happiness to my life in this way results in the creation of something far greater – joy.

We did eventually arrive at our camp that afternoon. The site was at the bottom of a deep side canyon, complete with a stream and an overhanging cliff that provided shade from the sun. We set up our gear under the overhang and prepared for the evening meal. As the sun set, the canyon was filled with a glowing red light that was being reflected off the towering vermillion cliffs that surrounded us. We sat there, in a circle, listening to the quiet. The depths of the Grand Canyon provide a level of quiet that I have never experienced before. The combination of the light and the quiet was mesmerizing. We all sat there in a deep state of peace. Eventually one of my friends began to speak. The words that sprang from his mouth were a remembrance of, unbelievably, a college broomball tournament. All of the people in our group had participated in that tournament, except for me. My friends added to the discussion with their memories of the tournament. I sat there, feeling the Complex well up inside me. Even after 30 years, the utterance of the word broomball could still create mind thought that would transport me to a place of fear and suffering.

But it was different this time. This time, I saw the Complex almost immediately. I became the Watcher, saw that the Complex was not me, returned to the present moment and then made the choice to be happy. Happy for the opportunity that broomball and the Complex had just brought to me. The opportunity to wake up; to become conscious. What an incredible gift. And that is where I find that happiness transmutes into something far greater – joy. Joy was in the returning, and subsequently being returned to, the present moment with my friends. A moment that included the ethereal light of the canyon sunset, the majestic cliffs around me and the love of close friends. Joy was in knowing that these incredible, wonderful people had given me the gift of opportunity and that I had come to be able to recognize it. Joy came from understanding and implementing the process to deliver myself from suffering.

## Inspiration

I cannot tell you how much more spectacularly beautiful the world has become since I started employing these teachings and techniques in my life. The world around me has become more vibrant than ever before. Positive synchronistic events happen more frequently. My suffering has been greatly reduced. I will tell you that I am not perfect in employing these techniques successfully all the time. I have found that, like so many other things, practice yields improvement. I have found that the more I practice these techniques, the more my suffering decreases, and the more my joy increases. The infusion of joy into my life provides inspiration and strong motivation for me to continue on this path.

I brought these teachings and techniques to my relationship with my mother and it has greatly enhanced our connection. My dad passed away many years ago which was prior to my understanding and learning many of these techniques. Based on how far our relationship had progressed at the time that he died, it would have been wonderful to see how far we could have gone. I remain grateful for the time that we had and for the positive, affirming relationship that we were able to create. I shall always be thankful for the love, understanding and acceptance that my parents have shown toward me.

## Manifestation

Recently I celebrated my fiftieth birthday by taking a trip out of state to do some skiing. I happened to be off skiing by myself one day, when I ran into a man that I had worked with for many years back in Seattle. Ours was strictly a professional relationship; we were not friends and I did not know much about his personal life. We had come across each other while having a beer on an outdoor deck at the base of the mountain – a fun and frolicking après ski atmosphere. It was a stunningly beautiful Colorado day with a cobalt blue sky overhead, the sun shining brightly and warmly and not a cloud to be seen. We made a toast to our pleasant and unlikely meeting here on this deck, so far away from our homes. We raised our pints into the air, the sun catching the little white bubbles rising through the copper colored sunlit beer, and toasted to our good fortune and gratitude for being in such a spectacular place. At that moment, a woman appeared at his side. He greeted her warmly and then introduced her to me as being his wife. They began to talk to me, and I made the decision to stop them. Music had started on the deck and the après ski revelry had become quite loud. I could not raise my voice enough to be heard above the noise and have conversation. I leaned closely into them so that they could hear my voice and explained to them that I could not talk any longer. They nodded their understanding, and we agreed that we would ski together the next day.

The next day's weather was a repeat of the day before – sunny, clear, bright with a sparkling blue sky. It was the end of the season and there were very few people skiing on the mountain – we practically had the place to ourselves. On one particular gondola ride, they questioned me about my voice and how it came to sound as it does. I told them the story of my journey with RRP. When I was done the wife looked at me with amazement and said, "Have you ever thought about writing down that story? I am a writer and that kind of story fascinates me from a writing perspective." I felt a wave of energy come over me as she finished those words. It felt like the Universe/God/Consciousness had tapped me on the shoulder and said, "Listen and Stay Open." I had never been a writer. I had never enjoyed writing. Writing was just something I had done because I had to, to get through school or work. But, I stayed open to what she was saying and to what was happening to me. I stayed open to the present moment and to what life was bringing me right then and there. She continued on by telling me that she had been a writer all her life and that she even had her own website dedicated to her writing. I continued to stay open. She said, "Ya know, you should think about doing it. All you have to do is sit down and just start writing." I felt the strength, power and depth of a force that I had heard referred to before as an Epiphany, come over me. Its message was simple. *You need to write. You need to write about your life experience.* I remained open. I did not let my mind close me down as it produced such thoughts as: "you don't know how to write, you are not a writer, you can't write well enough to do this." Those thoughts came forward, for sure, but I did not buy into them. I watched them, separated myself from them, became conscious of them and then made the choice to dismiss them and return to the present moment. The present moment that was filled with the energy of this epiphany. I remained open, sitting there in that gondola car, and just allowed the force of the epiphany to wash over me. It was my most concrete feedback yet of the power that comes forward when I stay open.

That power manifested this book – this life experience put into words. I hope it can give something; help someone else to reduce the amount of suffering in their life.

If you think or you feel that you have a Complex/Ego/Self that is causing you to suffer, try these techniques and see if they make a difference for you.

I hope this account of my journey thus far in this life can help someone else to become free. Free as I have started to become, *Free from My Self*.

# Appendix

I keep the following list at a place in my home where I can see it often. I have found that the more I practice these eight steps, the easier it becomes to recognize when my mind is causing me to suffer. The more I practice, the quicker I am able to catch the thoughts in my head *as they arise* and put an end to them if they are causing me to suffer. I put an end to them by coming back to the present moment.

----------------

If you feel that you are at unease or discontented in some way in your life, if you feel or know that you are suffering in some way, take the following steps:

1. Become the Watcher. Watch the thoughts in your head and the emotions that arise. Don't judge or resist the thoughts and emotions. Just accept them as they are and watch them.

2. As you watch, realize that the thoughts in your head and the emotions that are produced are not you. Realize that the voice in your head is not who you are.

3. As you watch with acceptance and without judgment or resistance, notice the space between you, the Watcher, and your thoughts and emotions.

4. Watch that space. Watch the thoughts and emotions beyond that space and realize that you are watching as your true essence. You are watching from *your being* and not from your Complex/Ego/Self. You have become conscious. You have woken up.

5. Then make your choice, from this place of consciousness, as to how to proceed in life. If you wish to not become involved in the thoughts and emotions that you observe and the suffering that they are causing you, make the conscious choice to return to the present moment. The present moment is the way out.

6. Practice present moment awareness.

7. Practice acceptance, non-resistance and non-judgment of that present moment, be *open*, and then move forward from that place.

8. Practice gratitude. Be grateful that you have found a way out of suffering and grateful for the abundance of life all around you.

# References

Tolle, Eckhart. (1997) The Power of Now: A Guide to Spiritual Enlightenment. Vancouver, B.C.: Namaste Publishing.

Tolle, Eckhart. (2005) A New Earth: Awakening to Your Life's Purpose. New York, NY: Penguin Publishing.

Singer, Michael A. (2007) The Untethered Soul: The Journey Beyond Yourself. Oakland, CA: New Harbinger Publications, Inc., Petaluma, CA: Noetic Books.

www.ingramcontent.com/pod-product-compliance
Lightning Source LLC
Chambersburg PA
CBHW050627300426
44112CB00012B/1696